To Teach or Not To Teach

A Collaboration Book of Educators Sharing Stories and Tips on the Controversial Topic of Leaving or Staying in the Classroom

Shanine Alessia Young
Tiffaney "Fenyx Blue" Washington
Aaliyah M Burgess
Dr. Natasha Myla
Delisha Easley
Kimberly Simons
Brittney Bolden
Monica Tookes
Stephanie Sanders
Yolanda Dudley
Dr. Dashia Andrews
Martina Britt Yelverton
Angela Taylor

Copyright © 2022 by Reaching While Teaching LLC

All rights reserved. This book or any portion thereof may not be reproduced or used in any manner whatsoever without the express written permission of the publisher except for the use of brief quotations in a book review.

Printed in the United States of America

First Printing, 2022

ISBN: 978-1-7379081-9-7

Edited & Formatted by Show Your Success

Published by Reaching While Teaching LLC

Table of Contents

Foreword v

Introduction
By: Shanine Alessia Young 1

Shanine Alessia Young 3

Tiffaney "Fenyx Blue" Washington 15

Aaliyah M Burgess 29

Dr. Natasha Myla 39

Delisha Easley 51

Kimberly Simons 59

Brittney Bolden 67

Monica Tookes 75

Stephanie Sanders 85

Yolanda Dudley 93

Dr. Dashia Andrews 101

Martina Britt Yelverton 109

Angela Taylor 117

Conclusion 129

Bonus Material 133

Business Listings 137

Foreword

Shanine Alessia Young's ground-breaking anthology *To Teach or Not To Teach* comes at a time when educators, both inside and outside of the classroom, are increasingly becoming more aware of their purpose in education and whether that involves classroom teaching. The great thing is that all educators have different journeys. There is no "right" way to be an educator. The purpose of this book is to guide readers through the process for their own understanding using examples from other educators.

I was first introduced to Shanine a few years ago through her engaging social media content and upbeat personality. Her first book, *Reaching While Teaching*, was the kind of book that I wish I had while I was teaching—inspirational, practical, and faith-based. As a former teacher, I related to Shanine's teaching experience and could tell that she was a passionate educator with a genuine heart for her students. Some educators realize that they have a calling outside of the classroom. I have transitioned to becoming a filmmaker focused on films about K-12 public education issues. Shanine has become a full-time entrepreneur—teaching on a new level through her books, coaching, and speaking.

The Covid-19 pandemic caused many educators to question their purpose as they learned new systems, acquired remote learning skills, and managed their mental health. The pandemic exposed many of the previous issues in the education system. Many educators began to critically analyze why they made the decision to pursue the education field, what their professional goals were, and whether they intended to stay in the profession.

To Teach or Not To Teach explores what some may consider to be a controversial topic. However, it's a necessary topic that needs to be discussed. Readers may begin to ask themselves questions as it relates to their own personal freedom and how they serve in the world. The book allows educators to hear from others with different perspectives and positions. There are strategies included in the book to help work through the decision-making process regardless of whether the intent is to stay in the classroom for a couple of years, a few years, or for your entire career. Prepare to be enlightened!

Stacie McClam, Educator & Filmmaker
Founder of School Dismissed
www.schooldismissed.com

Introduction
By: Shanine Alessia Young

Have you ever sat down and contemplated a decision you needed to make? Has that decision ever been regarding your job or what you do for a living? Before the pandemic, I never thought much about switching careers or leaving my job as a full-time English teacher. I had six years of teaching experience under my belt, and I loved my students and loved the impact I was making.

I'm going to take you down memory lane with me. I remember the very first year I started teaching in 2014. A student by the name of Brandon told me, " Ms., do you know you are one of the best teachers I've ever had?" He was in 8th grade, and I couldn't help but smile because I knew I was making a difference. I brought so much creativity and fun into the classroom, and each year I fell in love with more and more students.

In 2019, after I had my first child, it was a little difficult to adjust to going back into the classroom since I had six months off to nurture her and raise her after she was born and I was so attached to my baby girl. As time went by, I noticed a few shifts and changes happening in education and especially in the inner city schools where I worked, but that did not discourage me. I kept showing up to work and showing up for my students, and I even published my very first book in 2020 called Reaching While Teaching: An Educator's Guide to Impacting & Transforming Lives. This book was inspired by my students and became an

Introduction

instant success. Writing this book ignited the spark I already had for entrepreneurship, and I went ahead and formed an LLC a few months after publishing my book.

Fast forward to 2021, my coaching business grew, and I continued to help more and more authors and entrepreneurs publish and market their books. I struggled for months contemplating whether I should continue to be a full-time educator. It took some time, but I finally realized that I will always be a teacher, whether I am teaching in or outside of the classroom. I'm sure many other educators around the world might have also asked themselves the question, To Teach or Not to Teach? Just know if that's you, then you are not alone.

If you are currently questioning if you should stay or leave the classroom, then this book is for you. This book has been on my heart for a while, and I decided to create this book and bring together several educators from all over the world so they can address how you can overcome obstacles and thrive no matter what final decision you make regarding staying in the classroom or leaving. I chose to teach outside of the four walls of the classroom and embark upon the journey of entrepreneurship. This is just my story; you might have considered teaching, or maybe you are currently in the classroom. As you read these pages, your eyes will be opened, you will be encouraged, and you will be empowered to be a part of the change that your world needs to see by honing your skills and expertise so you can continue to provide value and create an impact by building your legacy.

Shanine Alessia Young

Instagram - Reachingwhileteaching
Facebook - reachingwhileteaching
Linkedin - shanine-alessia-young
www.books2impact.com

Shanine Alessia Young is your favorite Author Coach, Keynote Speaker, and Certified Educator who is passionate about teaching entrepreneurs, students and educators how to increase their confidence and impact. She shows entrepreneurs how to publish and market books that will grow their businesses. She is the CEO of Reaching While Teaching, LLC. Shanine shows you how to turn your story and expertise into a published book and also shows entrepreneurs how to create content that increases their visibility and exposure, thus increasing their revenue. She has been featured in FOX, Voyage Miami, and several other news outlets. Reaching While Teaching others is the goal and her business exists to educate, empower and equip individuals to live their best life possible using their God-given gifts, talents, and abilities.

Stay connected with Shanine on social media IG: @reachingwhileteaching or Reaching While Teaching on FB.

Share what you do and your experience with education.

I'm currently a full-time entrepreneur with over eight years of teaching experience. I've been dubbed "Your Favorite Author Coach" because I enjoy helping entrepreneurs turn their stories and expertise into published books so they can increase their impact while increasing their income. As far as my experience with education, after I graduated from college, I joined a program called City Year, a service program where I was able to work inside inner-city schools and provide mentorship and reading interventions to struggling students. After serving for about a year, I fell in love with the students and wanted to stay in the classroom. I studied for the teaching certification tests so that I could teach English to middle and high school students, and I passed every single one of them. Shortly after, I started the journey as an 8th-grade English/Language Arts teacher in Florida. While in education, I've held many roles, such as Poetry Club Sponsor, Step Team Coach, Grade Level Leader, Department Head, and the list goes on. My very first book, which I self-published in 2020, was all about my experience in education and equipping other teachers on how to transform and impact lives in and out of the classroom.

The pandemic helped me to value family time more and I truly enjoyed working from home. In 2021, once we started entering back into the classrooms I no longer felt the joy I once felt and I was longing for a change. I decided to take a break from teaching. My family and I relocated to Georgia toward the end of the school year, and I was able to take almost a year off from teaching and fully focus on my business and raising our one-year-old daughter. At this time, I was still figuring things out and debating on if I wanted to return to the classroom because I enjoyed teaching, but I really felt God was calling me to do so much more. In Dec 2021, I returned as a full-time teacher for the last six months of school and in a whole nother state! Man, talk about a culture shock. It was extremely rough at first, but after the first two months, I got the hang of it and stuck it out because I knew the students had gone through so much and so many changes before I got there. During this time, I pushed even harder in my business and stayed up many late nights after work working on business plans and lesson plans because I was on a mission. I plan to continue to be involved in the education space, but I plan to do it on my terms. I specifically love working with teacherpreneurs and helping them tap into multiple streams of income through book publishing and book leveraging.

What is one thing you love the most about being a teacher, or if you are no longer teaching, what do you love most about your new profession?

Although I'm not currently in the classroom, I'm still teaching. I teach master classes, I visit schools and teach students socioemotional skills and I have a Books 2 Impact program where I help entrepreneurs learn some of the best ways to publish and market their books. I also teach bi-weekly training sessions in our inner circle mentoring group for business owners who are trying to grow their businesses in regard to marketing, exposure, and funding. I love that I have the freedom to travel and speak at different events without needing to request a day off. I am able to spend more time with my daughter and husband. As an Author Coach, what brings me the most joy is helping people bring their vision to life. People come to me with a vision of a book idea, and the fact that I get to see their faces once they hold their book in their hand for the first time always makes me feel so proud. Helping people make an impact and increase their income by creating something they are passionate about is a huge win for me.

I love that I am not stationary. My students are all over the world. I'm able to teach in a virtual setting some days and in a physical setting on other days. With this new journey I am on, I'm also able to make a bigger impact on the educational system because some of the books I have published and some of the books my clients have published are now being used inside of classrooms all over the world. Recently, I traveled out of state and taught a 6th grade class from my best selling book "Freedom Over Fear". I helped show them how to achieve some of their goals and shared a few financial literacy tips and tricks. To be a teacher means to inspire and that's what I love the most.

What are some challenges you've faced as a teacher?

I honestly don't know any teacher who hasn't faced challenges. If I could think of the top challenges I faced being a teacher, I would have to say being required to do something just to follow a mandate. There were so many unpaid trainings we had to attend which usually meant there was a new mandate or requirement we had to follow and it became a challenge when these requirements were not beneficial to our students. I remember several times my whole team voicing their opinion on a certain matter, and we all got ignored because it was a mandate given by the district, so the administration didn't want to go against it. Also, it's very challenging to keep our students inspired and motivated when we are forced to constantly test them over and over. It seems like every year, they add a new test or assessment, and sometimes a student can take up to three tests in one week which to me is a bit ridiculous.

Something else that I've had to deal with was chasing down parents. Those students who sometimes give you the most headache tend to have parents who change their number every week or do not have updated contact information in the system. I remember having to call several people in the office to get accurate information and it always felt like I was going in circles. One more challenge that I know is necessary but I still hated because of what this world has become is the code red drills for active shooters. At first, the students took it seriously, but as time progressed, many kids got so used to these drills that they would play, and we would have to share closets with other classes and have to try and manage other students who weren't even in our classes sometimes.

If you could give two tips to a new teacher reading this book, what would they be?

Tip #1 would be to find one thing every day to give thanks for. No matter how difficult the class might be, it doesn't matter if you didn't get a chance to update your lesson plans. There's always something that you can be grateful for. I would say starting off your morning with this attitude and even ending your day with this attitude can be extremely helpful for any teacher. There might be four kids misbehaving while eight of them are listening and completing their work. Give thanks for those eight that are actually on task and listening. There are so many things that we can let upset us on a minute-to-minute basis as a teacher, but I have found giving thanks for the positive things you see happening can change your whole day.

Tip#2 would be to get to know your students' likes and dislikes. Get to know your students so that you can really understand them better and it will be easier to teach them when you do this. Always infuse activities that will allow you to learn a little bit more about your students and make sure they are aware that you truly care about them. In my very first book, "Reaching While Teaching: An Educator's Guide to Impacting and Transforming Lives," I share specific examples and instances of how I made it a priority to really get to know my students. What I found is students find it hard to learn from someone they do not like. Now every student, of course, won't feel like you're their favorite teacher, but they should still respect you and feel like you care.

If you stayed in the classroom, what motivated you to stay, and what advice would you provide to someone who was in a similar position? Or If you left the classroom, what influenced that decision, and how did you decide your next steps?

I left the classroom because I felt like God was calling me to tap into my teaching skills but on a whole nother level. During my seventh year as a teacher, I still enjoyed teaching my kids, but I felt like there was something else that I should be doing and that it was time to leave the classroom, but God kept telling me, "not yet." He was preparing me and getting me ready. I had to spend quality time with Him in order for me to know the next steps to take. Once He showed me a glimpse of the plan, I trusted and followed His direction every step of the way. From leaving a career of over eight years to moving to a whole new state and buying our second home where we had little to no family to help with our toddler, it took a lot of faith. God told me to write down what I wanted to see come from this business of mine, and everything I wrote on my prayer wall upon moving came to pass because I took things one step at a time and followed His lead.

Something else that influenced my decision to leave the classroom was my family. During this time of getting clarity on my next move, I knew I wanted to be more involved in my daughter's education and social-emotional support. I did not want her to be in daycare for 9 hours a day. The pandemic reminded me of the importance of family time and why you should do all that you can to get as much family time as you can get. Spending those extra hours and days at home with my daughter and husband brought me so much joy. These early moments in a child's life are crucial, and you can't get these moments back.

So if you are taking notes on my journey of leaving the classroom as a full time teacher, these are basically the steps:

1. Pray and wait on clarity if this is the move for you
2. Write down your reason for leaving and your vision
3. Do it as a side hustle first (get your feet wet and be sure this is what you want)
4. Write down your exit strategy (Set a timetable, start saving money, set your S.M.A.R.T. Goals)
5. Take the leap of faith and leave your 9-5 or teaching career

Why is a book like this needed?
This book is truly one of a kind because it's filled with so many different perspectives from teachers who are still in the trenches and teachers who have left the classroom. This book will help individuals who are considering entering the classroom because after reading each chapter, they'll be able to make a more informed decision. This book will also help those in educational leadership Sometimes textbooks don't always include up-to-date, real-life experiences. You are able to hear the real and raw truth that sometimes doesn't always get voiced. Hearing from former and current teachers who have experience in different grade levels, states and subjects is something I wish I could have

experienced before I started teaching. A book like this is rare and priceless.

Based on your experience, what would you say to a teacher who is unsure about whether to stay or leave the classroom?

I would say you need to know your **BIG WHY**.

If you were to stay, why would you stay? If you were to leave, why would you leave?

Whichever reason is the most important to you and connects to your big why, lean toward that. Your **BIG WHY** is the reason for doing what you do and why you wake up each day. When you truly understand what your driving force is, this will help you make the right decision. For example, if you were considering leaving the classroom because you realize you have a strong desire to impact your student's parents and you want to help them become more financially literate, then you have to be honest with yourself. If you stay, ask yourself if you are able to fulfill this desire of yours. I realized that my BIG WHY was related to helping people use their voices to impact others through books. I was torn for a long time because by teaching English/Language arts, I'm helping my students with writing, and when we do journaling, they are able to share their stories as well, but I felt as though I was drawn toward book publishing and it was a greater passion because I could have more freedom with it. I knew I would be able to help others create generational wealth for their family. Sometimes it takes a while to really get clear on what you want, but once your BIG WHY keeps knocking at your door and you don't feel peace unless you pursue it, then you will know what decision to make.

If you had the power to change something in the education system, what would it be and why?

I would probably ensure the government is less involved with what goes on in the classroom. I would make sure they stop asking so much of teachers and administrators. So many mandates and tests continue to be enforced on students, and it takes so much away from the profession, and it becomes less enjoyable for the teachers and the students. The federal government should step up in funding because plenty of schools don't have the resources it needs to flourish. High-poverty districts tend to frequently get fewer dollars per student than low-poverty districts. Change needs to happen because the way the education system is headed is not in the best interest of our students.

What is your favorite quote?

"Tell me and I forget. Teach me and I remember. Involve me and I learn"- Benjamin Franklin.

Acknowledgments

Stacie McClam, @staciemcclam, www.SchoolDismissed.com
Bridgette & Ericka, @b.e._connected, www.beconnectedconsulting.com
Emily Bolhuis, @emilyballhouse, emilyballhouse
Todernesia Ford-Carter, @Educator_Coach_T
Philip Ak, @philipak418, www.philipak.com
Emily Ballhouse, @emilyballhouse, EmilyBallhouse.com
Sherine Isom, @Sherysom
Terrence Isom
Chantal Jennings, @ChantalJennings7

Nicole Lee, @Toldbynik, www.toldbynik.com

Abyon McInnis, @abyonausar, www.AbyonAusar.com

Amber Mitchell, @ambersaffirmations, www.ambersaffirmations.com

Charles Osuji, @keysdreamz, www.kingdomkeysmentoring.org

Caline Serafin, @cay_serafine

Silvana Spence, @Mrs.s4success, www.silsteps4success.com

Stephanie Williams, @steph.speaks, www.destinedtoconquer.com

Toi Witcher, @toi.Shanelle, www.visionheirymood.com

Jordan Young, @Jyoungsfl, Jyoungsfl.com

Demetrius Huckabee, @4thseal_tvnetwork

Kevin NiBlack

Carlene Wright, @wrightencouragement,

Lorna Smiley

Renee Lovekids, @reneelovekids, www.reneelovekids.com

Darrian Tanner, @teachmstanner, www.amentorforteachers.com

Samantha Jasmin

Tiffaney "Fenyx Blue" Washington

Instagram - fenyxblueink
Linkedin - fenyxblueink
fenyxblueink.wixsite.com

Former Teacher of the Year Fenyx Blue has served as an instructional coach, mentor, and leader for her school district. Blue is a best-selling author and has penned a book of poetry entitled The Blue Ink Movement, two children's books called Cash's Money Ties and Worth the Weight: A Rare Gem, and two YA novels named Who Failed Johnny? and Battle of The Bullies. Her publishing company, WISDOM Works, LLC, seeks to help people to write, publish and share their art with the community. In her two decades in education, Blue has created, led, and sponsored several clubs for youth. She currently speaks to audiences of all ages on financial literacy, wellness, bullying prevention, and education. Blue created a club called Team Bully-Free Forever to help end bullying of all forms and to empower students to become upstanders in their communities. She directs a youth anti-drug program called Snowflake that helps students to solve problems, build relationships and make positive choices. Blue has sponsored a poetry club of junior high students that went on to the final rounds of The Louder Than a Bomb competition, where they competed among high school students. With the support of other educators, she developed DIVAS (Daughters Inspiring Values and Sisterhood) to build bonds between middle and high school girls and prepare them to be productive citizens.

B.L.U.E. (Bold, Loving, Unapologetic, and Evolving) is the word that best describes Tiffaney Washington, AKA Ms. Fenyx Blue.

Share what you do and your experience with education.

According to my mother, I used to teach my stuffed animals and dolls. Mom says I even taught my cousins lessons to help them in school. I invented games for them to play. So I guess I've been a teacher for a very long time. In fact, when I went to college, I met a young lady who couldn't write an essay. She had made it through her entire school career and was not prepared for college. After working with her to develop the skill of writing, I learned that I wanted to become a teacher because I saw how impactful teaching can be on someone's life. That one skill was going to help her for life. I fell in love with teaching right then and there.

So my experiences with education have been very positive, and I've taken that love for education into how I am as an educator right now. Currently, I am an instructional coach who helps and supports teachers to grow as mindful, dynamic professionals.

So I've been teaching for over two decades, grades six through twelve, and now I coach kindergarten through eighth-grade teachers in all subject areas. So even though I've been an English Language Arts teacher for the majority of my career, I now have the opportunity to serve in all subjects in my school district. I'm also a mentor, director of many activities, and an active member of the leadership team.

So I've worn all the educational caps except the administrator one, mostly because I like to stay in the classroom. I love working with the teachers and students, so that's why I haven't quite put that cap on. I've been involved with curriculum and I've been a Teacher of the Year from my school district, which was one of the greatest honors that I've had. The final thing that I'd like to say about my experiences with education is to share one of my best experiences with education, and that is when my own student came back to the school district to let me know that she had started her own education program. She was formerly a struggling reader, but she had developed a program to help all students learn. With the help of my principal, she gave me an award for the impact that I had on her life. She surprised me in front of my entire class. This is just one memorable, positive experience with education. I'm so proud to be a teacher and now a teacher of teachers.

What is one thing you love the most about being a teacher, or if you are no longer teaching, what do you love most about your new profession?

I love many things about being a teacher, but there's a quote by Robert Heinlein that says, "when *one teaches, two learn.*" So I guess the thing that I love most about being a teacher is that it constantly stretches me as a human being and learner. In order to teach others to be their best, you have to be at your best.

It's like waking up to a challenge each and every day. I'm constantly learning from my students and building relationships with them because I love working with human beings who are going to be our future citizens in our world. I enjoy that aspect. They're going to be the future doctors, pilots, entrepreneurs, and teachers. And they teach me. They teach me how to dance. They teach me the newest tech and terms. For now, they keep me forever young. The teachers inspire me and show me new ways to reach kids each day. Being in multiple classrooms as a coach each day is like taking hundreds of teaching classes a year. I can't help but walk away with more tools in my teacher toolkit that I can share with my fellow educators. And so, despite the many challenges that there are with education, I think the positive is you get to stretch yourself and become the best version of yourself daily.

What are some challenges you've faced as a teacher?

The good thing about the teacher tribe is we experience many similar challenges. So there have been a lot of challenges. When you talk about the over two decades that I've experienced, the first one that comes to mind, though, is when I first started teaching and was placed in an academy. That's what they called it. But basically, it was the students who struggled behaviorally and academically. They were all placed in one school, isolated from other students, and had many challenges, from mental health to bad environments and struggles with their parents. Can you imagine how they felt being kicked out of their original school and placed in an "Academy," but knowing it's because of their past, their lack of skills, or their home circumstances? And so trying to get those scholars to know who they were and that they had potential was one of my biggest challenges as a brand-new teacher. We made it through by building self-esteem, reaching out to uninvolved parents, and creating the most engaging lessons and activities possible for the students. Their organization, math, and reading skills grew. They experienced years of growth in months, but it was very challenging.

In addition to those academic and behavioral challenges, there's *the challenge of burnout*, and not for myself, because I've had many strategies, but my empathy makes me experience the challenges of many of my peers leaving the profession, being burnt out, and having to continue to persevere. I've had students who've dealt with everything from divorce and death, but I've also dealt with the loss of apparently frustrated teachers. These were Teachers who I called colleagues, friends, or mentees. It's become a mission of mine to help students and teachers.

So basically, I would say that the biggest challenges that I faced were those with both students and those frustrated teachers that I've worked alongside in my school district and, of course, the parents who kind of hover too much or are ghosts and are invisible, one or the other. Parents, students, and my fellow teachers have challenged me over the years.

If you could give two tips to a new teacher reading this book, what would they be?

My first teacher tip would be that *you have to take care of yourself.* I think the key to my longevity in this profession is that I know that the most important person in the room is that teacher because the teacher is the one who's going to reach those students. And so even though the quote says that as teachers, we light candles, if your candle isn't lit, then you are not going to be able to light the candles of others. They say we teachers pour from our cups to other students, but if you have an empty cup, you're not going to be able to pour into others. We must learn to pour from the overflow. Our cups must be full and overflowing.

I believe that you have to do that. Self-care.

What do you enjoy? What are your hobbies?

Are you getting massages?

Are you getting facials?

Are you going for walks?

Are you taking care of your mental health?

Are you spending time with your family?

Are you reading, writing, or doing whatever brings you joy? Traveling brings me joy. The beach is my happy place. You need to have that. So when you have those difficult moments, when you are forced to lead and take care of students, you're able to do that and be a role model for them so that they see you in your best space and you can help them to be the best version of themselves. Happy teachers are contagious, so they make happy students.

The second tip that I would give to teachers is that *you need to know your resources in your school district.* Have a community, a tribe. Don't think that you're an island. I love the beach, but I know that I'm not an island. I know sometimes, when we go into our classrooms, we think that it's an island and we are in control. We're kind of the queens and kings of that world that we're in. But in order to survive in this, you need to extend beyond that and build your tribe in your community. Who are the custodians, the secretaries, and the other teachers around your school world? Get to know them. Learn from them. If they are toxic, go global. Now, we live in a global social media society that you can reach in contact with when you have those low points in your career. And you need to learn from their experience. The veterans that are in the field, maybe they know about a yoga program, or they know a counselor or a social worker. They know someone that could help you to get money or discounts as a teacher for those things that you might need to have solved, those problems that you feel you have; they may have the solution. So when you have a tribe and a community that's around you, and you use them as resources, and you give back to them, then you won't drown.

I think sometimes we think we're on that island, but don't forget that people are our life jackets and there are lifeboats. If we actually just reach out to them, they'll save us. Stop drowning silently. Stop suffering alone. Reach out to those teachers who consider themselves to be lifeguards on duty.

If you stayed in the classroom, what motivated you to stay, and what advice would you provide to someone who was in a similar position? Or if you left the classroom, what influenced that decision, and how did you decide your next steps?

So I definitely stayed in the classroom, and now I'm in other people's classrooms as well. And what motivated me to do that is my students over the years, those students that return to say thank you, to tell you how they've developed as human beings or in their careers, the random emails I've received, the letters, the phone calls. Because of these acts of appreciation, I know that my impact is going beyond me. It's going to other generations. I had the pleasure of hanging out with a former student just last night at Open House, and she showed me her business card. She had her daughter with her, and she was like, this teacher impacted me, and she introduced me that way. She said, "She's my favorite teacher." And so I know that as a teacher, the impact that you have, it goes on past that child. I taught her mom to read, and now she's teaching her own daughter to read, and it goes beyond that.

So I'm motivated by the impact that I've been able to have and the gifts of giving to others. And I know that most likely, just like my dad's favorite teacher Ms. Cannon impacted him and then he impacted me. And now I'm impacting my children. Or how the words of my former teacher Mr. Torrence telling me that I would one day be a teacher and that I should have continued to play on repeat in my mind and to impact me. The longevity and the impact of a teacher never dies. You live forever. So the advice would be to think with that end in mind and to know that begin with the end in mind. In the end, your impact never ends.

As Covey says in his book 7 Habits of *Highly Effective Pe*ople, begin with the end. The advice would be to know that it's not just about today. You're going to have some rough days today but think about tomorrow. And those tomorrows will help you to get through. And even those tomorrows when you're no longer here, your impact will continue to grow. So try to focus on that. Have a vision board. Have a vision. See it. Then, be it.

Why is a book like this needed?

Unfortunately, you don't see a book titled to Be an Engineer or not to Be an Engineer or To Be a Lawyer or not to be a Lawyer, an athlete or not to be an athlete, right? Because in our society, those professions or being a celebrity, they're celebrated, and they're appropriately compensated for what they do. Whereas with teachers, that's not necessarily the case. And so you have some of the most brilliant minds out there, people with great hearts who are full of potential, who find themselves at a crossroad wondering, should I do this? Should I stay or should I go? And it's sad because many of them are called to do it. They're meant to do it. They're supposed to do it. It's what they were created to do. But they have to consider things like burnout or compensation or being disrespected. And so they find themselves wondering, should I do this job? Should I remain where I am tolerated and not celebrated? And so a book like this is so valuable because it's going to allow them to see both sides of the situation, why should I stay or why shouldn't I stay as a teacher? And so if you are gifted and you're gifted to give, but you're wondering, well, should I continue to do this, this book will help you to explore that. And if you are thinking, hey, I like to use my gifts elsewhere, this book will help you to explore that as well. It will give those undecided teachers a chance to hear from those experts who have been in the field. This book will allow others to learn from someone's experience. So the book is necessary because it's going to give permission to teachers to weigh the pros and the cons of their profession. And it's a reminder of how important that choice to teach is for future generations. So I hope the teachers will choose to teach.

Based on your experience, what would you say to a teacher who is unsure about whether to stay or leave the classroom?

What would our world be like if there were no teachers? Every profession is built on a lesson, and I would remind them of that. No matter if teachers are called trainers or guides or mentors or gurus. We have so many names for teachers. No matter what you call them, their calling is valuable.

So I would tell them if they have been called to teach, it's a special call. You are a unique person. Most likely, you're gifted, and you're talented. You have what's inside of you that can impact future generations. If you choose not to, then you are leaving the world without that gift. So a road that may have been smooth may now be rocky because the world is waiting on you. You may be waiting on the world, but the world is waiting on you. I would share a story with them about how my father could not read, but he had a teacher who believed in him. And he decided to go to her and say he was basically going to give up on the whole school thing. She poured into him. She used every talent that she could to teach him how to read in his class as well. She was also one of the first African American teachers in his school, so she represented possibility to him. She went over and beyond for her students until they learned.

And he had never had that before. And so that one teacher who believed in him helped him to become a graduate. And then, of course, my dad taught me how to read. And now, from that, not only can I read, but I've read aloud to my children and my students. I've written many books, and my own children are honor students and gifted readers. So one teacher's impact and decision not to leave the classroom has forever impacted our family. And so that is what you as a teacher will be missing out on. And I hope that a teacher would choose to stay in their position and choose the path that will impact many paths moving forward. (BTW: That teacher has a street named after her in Markham, Illinois, but I can't promise you will have streets named after you...I'm just saying it could happen... lol)

If you had the power to change something in the education system, what would it be and why?

If I had that magic wand to change the education system, I probably would be hoping for like three wishes. But if I only get one thing, I would wish that everyone in education had the power of empathy. I think that one of the things that are missing from our school communities is that we see each other as enemies or we don't see each other at all. There's a lot of finger-pointing between students, parents, teachers, administration, and the community. And so we need that empathy instead of people feeling as if they're victims, knowing that they can be problem solvers with power. So that one day, when teachers decide to have empathy for their students and they see them as their own children, then they'll teach better. And when students can see teachers as their loved ones and not just that lady or that man, then they'll be better learners. They will come to class prepared and be more respectful. When the administration sees their staff as partners who are their equals and respect the gifts that they have, then we'll have better communities. And our community sees that we're all developing. We're not there yet, but we're all on this journey together. If we had empathy, we could truly experience the true possibilities of education.

I'm a teacher who wishes she could teach the world a lesson on empathy.

Education was always meant to be a *we*. It was what we were doing as a collective to make our citizenry better and smarter. And once we decide to actually see things from other people's points of view, we'll have a better education system. Until then, we just have to focus on ourselves and try to be the best version of ourselves that we can be and have empathy for each person that we meet. That is a power that we all already possess, the power to decide who we will be. I wish we all would decide to choose to be empathetic. "Could a greater miracle happen than for us to look through each other's eyes for an instant?" -Henry David Thoreau

Acknowledgments

Zaneta Adams, @Zadams_1
Jerry Barnes, @westsidebrotha2000
Melanie Bell
Terrence Brooks, @thereal_tahj
Sonia Cobb
Daphne Cooper

Arlene Dewey

Depriessa Fikes

Pat Finley

Amy Gehrt, @shuggehrt

Lovie Gordon

Shawnda Jackson, @Lifebeautycoach, www.lifesbeautifuldiamonds.com

Alice Johnson, , N/A

Bernice Johnson, @Bernice.johnson.376

Jeffrey Kaess, @Ohhidro

Arnee Love

Michelle McKay

Evita McNeil

Emily Nicotra, @Mrsnicotraela

Lisa Nicotra

Aja Parker, @parker_aja

Ursula Parris, @ursulasjourney

Tara Peacock

Toyas Rudolph, @tnrudolph

Kwalfle Scott-Bradley

Mary Jean, Smith

Stan Smith

Toni Sproch

Khadijah Washington, @dijah_didit

Legacy Washington, @legacyy.y

Michelle Wisniewski

Alyssa Zajack, @alyssazaj

Andrew Snorton

Annette Mays

Anthony Canady, Jr.

Anthony Westbrooks
Arthur "Moochie" Johnson
Dori Elmore
Edmon Gordon III
Iris Carey
Jamaica Canady
Latarius Washington, Jr.
Monica Lacey
Naadirah Muhammad
Patricia Wilson
Sylvia Winfrey
Thelma Conner
Tracy Williamson
Zachary "Ace" Gordon

Aaliyah M Burgess

Instagram - theorganizedcreator
Linkedin - organizedcreator
www.organizedcreator.com

Aaliyah Burgess-Richburg is from Columbia, SC. She graduated from Georgia Southern University with a degree in Elementary and Special Education. Aaliyah has always loved working with kids, even as a kid herself. The only thing she knew to be to continue working with youth was becoming a teacher. She thought becoming a teacher would fulfill her career dreams. However, things do not always go as planned. Aaliyah tried virtual teaching, substituting, museum camps, summer camps, church child aide, and after-school programs. Every time, there was something that was not satisfying enough for her to continue, whether it be money, operations, or a change in location. Today, she is letting God lead her path to find her purpose on her career journey. Aaliyah still wants to impact youth which is why she is obtaining a master's degree in Youth Development Leadership. She knows that youth need to have strong, positive home environments, communities, and people in their lives, and she wants to support these areas so we can raise up a greater generation. Until then, Aaliyah wants you to remember to love yourself because no one else will. This goes for loving yourself when it comes to family, jobs, friends, and anything that requires your time, energy, and effort.

Share what you do and your experience with education.

Life has a funny way of working out. I am a stay-at-home mom and entrepreneur, which, if you had asked me five years ago where I thought I'd be, this is not what I imagined. As an entrepreneur, I am a virtual assistant. I support educators and former educators with businesses, and I'm working with God to create another stream of income that aligns more with my purpose. Stay tuned for that purpose in the next episode of *What is Aaliyah Up To Now?*

I would have to say my experience with education is extensive. As far as my background before actually going into official teaching, I've been working with kids since I can remember. Ever since I was a little girl, people have told me children naturally gravitate to me, and I'd be an amazing teacher, so when it came time to think about what I wanted to be when I grew up, teaching was the only thing on my mind.

Instead of going to "big church," I helped with the children's church. If I couldn't help in the children's church, I would work in the nursery. I've worked with children through summer camps, museum camps, volunteer tutoring, and so much more. Kids have my heart, so anytime I could be with them, I was right there. I officially got into the teacher world in 2020 during the Pandemic, which has been very interesting. I started as a 2nd-grade teacher at a charter school. Many schools did not want to risk bringing kids back in, so we started off virtually. During this time, I was pregnant, so when everyone else went back in person, I had the opportunity to keep teaching from home, and it definitely had its challenges. Then, I taught 1st grade as a long-term substitute and fell in love. Afterward, I taught K-2nd grade as a summer camp and after-school teacher.

What is one thing you love the most about being a teacher, or if you are no longer teaching, what do you love most about your new profession?

I'm still a substitute teacher for our public county schools, and I also sub for an after-school program that I worked with. My favorite thing about being a teacher is the kids. I love building relationships with them and seeing where they come from and why they are the way they are. I enjoy watching them grow and have aha moments. It's honestly the whole child for me. The children make the experience of a teacher worthwhile.

But I also have to say that since I'm no longer full-time teaching, the thing that I love the most is my freedom. I don't have to wake up at the booty crack of dawn and go be on somebody's clock. I don't have to do all this extra paperwork and wear a million and one hats for over 20 different children at once. Whenever I teach kids now, I can teach them however I want to teach them. As far as my new profession, it allows me to explore life with my daughter and figure out what God has in store for me. I always dreamed of a chance to homeschool my kids and make education what I expect it to be. Now, I have that opportunity… as long as money keeps coming in some kind of way.

What are some challenges you've faced as a teacher?

Let's see, *boundaries with parents.* At the first school I ever taught at, we had to talk to 100% of our students' parents. Every single parent, every single week. That meant that some days I was talking to parents at 6:00 in the evening because they didn't get off work until that time. Or I had parents who would text me at very late hours throughout the night. As a first-time teacher, it was difficult not to respond back because I felt obligated to.

Another challenge was all the additional work. I was virtual, and it was new to everyone how to operate keeping track of students' engagement and progress. The school was trying to find systems that worked, but we just kept getting things added onto our plate, but nothing was being taken off.

My last challenge was work-life balance. I became so consumed in trying to make this new take on school a great experience for my students by applying what I learned during college and what type of teacher I wanted to live up to be. It got to the point that my boyfriend would call me while he was at work to check on me, and I would be deep in lesson plans and prep for the day well into 7 o'clock at night. It took me being so exhausted and realizing how much time I was spending in one spot to hold myself accountable for stopping all work once I clocked out. It was difficult because this meant I had to spend every chance I got during the day to finish things for my babies and work to be turned into administration.

If you could give two tips to a new teacher reading this book, what would they be?

For sure, just *come in and be you.* I think a lot of times, we have these high set expectations for ourselves and opinions from other people. And if you don't want to be that person that goes all out and decorates your classroom, you don't have to do that. If you want to create lessons that are more interactive than your team, go for it. Just do what's best for you and what's best for your students.

Tip number two; *definitely set boundaries with everybody, even your students.* Sometimes you have to have boundaries with your students because they can overstep things, not even realizing that they are doing it. Have boundaries with your administration. If there's given work that seems out of contract, don't feel as though you have to do it. Set that boundary before it's too late and they are always looking to you to do it. It's okay to say no. Have boundaries with coworkers. I've had coworkers who try to get deep into my personal business, and it's like, hey, we're here for the kids, and we ain't made it that far. In the long run, you'll be happy you set those boundaries from the jump.

If you stayed in the classroom, what motivated you to stay, and what advice would you provide to someone who was in a similar position? Or if you left the classroom, what influenced that decision, and how did you decide your next steps?

I left the classroom because I was pregnant in the first year that I taught. And the decision came along where I was like, I'm beyond stressed right now. I didn't want to have my daughter and potentially endure postpartum depression. So, I decided whenever I went on maternity leave, I was not coming back. It was the hardest decision. I contemplated it for months. I felt crazy to be leaving a school that paid the highest in the district and state. After getting over that, it just became trying to find my purpose, trying to find where I fit, trying to find what God has intentions for me to do in this world. And so that's why I kind of went back into the classroom as a substitute because that's all I knew, and it allowed me that freedom where I can come in as needed. I don't have to do everything that other teachers do, which is pretty sweet.

If you do find yourself in a similar position, just try to work different things out. See where you fit in the teaching world, and if the teaching world isn't it, find something else. Don't force it or the kids will be the ones who suffer.

Why is a book like this needed?

A book like this, first of all, I don't think I've ever read a book where there are teachers who are giving real-life experiences about what is actually going on in education or what they really feel and what they've gone through.

Also, this is a book authored by women of color, most importantly BLACK WOMEN, and so often, we don't get heard. So being able to hear the point of view of black women who are in the education system is very much needed because there are so many youths who are coming up now who are trying to figure out if education is for them, and the only resources they have are from Caucasian women or women of other descent. Don't forget representation matters, no matter what age.

The book is also needed because it not only gives other people who want to possibly go into teaching perspective, but it gives people who are not teaching our viewpoint and what we are really going through. Too often, I hear people talk down on teaching or think it's the easiest thing in the world. Teaching comes naturally to many, but when you are in a classroom, teaching is not the only job you have. You become a mom, a nurse, a therapist, a coach, a nutritionist, a mediator, and really an all-around superhuman just so your students can have the best learning experience and reach their fullest potential.

Based on your experience, what would you say to a teacher who is unsure about whether to stay or leave the classroom?

Pray. Pray. And Pray. During this time, I prayed until the wheels fell off. I did a lot of pros and cons. I talked it out with my boyfriend so much that he probably wanted to close his ears as soon as he heard the sound "tea" come out of my mouth. If this is your first year teaching, at least give it a chance. Give it a chance so you can say, I tried it, I did it, and I know for sure it's not for me.

If you've been in there for a little while, I really say try to talk it out, write a list of benefits to staying and leaving, try a different grade level, a new school, or maybe even a new district. It might be the environment you are in rather than teaching itself that has you on edge.

If you choose to leave the classroom but still have a love for kids, there are soooo many other ways to work with kids. However, when we get our degrees in education, we are only exposed to teaching in the classroom. Keep searching until you find what fits for you.

Now for those of you that find out you don't want to be reminded of teaching, explore your enjoyment from when you were younger. I forgot how much I loved graphic design and computer programming as a child that I never explored it. You may have been holding onto someone else's dream for you, and it's time to love yourself by doing what you want to do.

If you had the power to change something in the education system, what would it be and why?

Do I really have to choose just one? There is a lot I'd love to reform, but I'll stick to the one. The time frame for school. I'm talking about the time kids go in and leave to how time is spent in the classroom. I get that back in the day, it was made for school to fit the schedule of a parent who works. But I feel as though we have kids in school for far too long, and half the time, they're not even learning what we want them to learn because we're trying to cram things.

School should start later and not even be open as long as it is. Kids do not need 8 hours of school. It literally takes two to four hours a day to teach a child, depending on their age. The rest of the day can be spent exploring their community and getting real-life experiences instead of just being told about them. The way youth are being taught sets them up to cram and store information in their short-term memory so they can pass a test and never use it again.

If we want to raise youth to be well-adapted young adults and citizens, we have to make the application of the things they are learning mean more to them.

Acknowledgments

Macy Dykes
Sydne Hennings, @Impower_movememt, www.Impmvt.org
Debra Hornsby, @Fanissnic
Dena McComBs, @denamccombs, mccombs-notary.business.
   site
Patricia Richburg
Sparkle richburg, @msrichburg
William Richburg jr
Janella Shields, @JStillstanding
Lanetta Singleton, @nettas_on_ig
Sheila Stuckey, @sstuckey35
Tara Turner, @tara_turner_

Dr. Natasha Myla

Instagram - HawtHosting
Linkedin - drnatashamyla
www.HawtHosting.com

Dr. Natasha Myla is a mother of two sons, the CEO of Hawt Hosting, a Professional Speaker, and an inspiring author and devoted educator. She is on a mission to make a positive impact in the world of mentorship and empowering youths by guiding them into their God-given purpose. Her daily goal is to be intentional in pouring positivity into others. Dr. Myla started her career as a second-grade teacher who later taught various grade levels. Ten years later, she became an instructional curriculum coach at a low-performing school, which improved at the end of the school year. As an educator, her passion for empowering and mentoring both students and adult learners is indescribable. In her current position as one of the school district's Instructional Specialists, Dr. Myla has had the opportunity to teach thousands of elementary-level scholars and continued her journey in supporting hundreds of educators across the school district. While supporting schools, she was able to build and focus on her emcee business, Hawt Hosting, and had the opportunity to collaborate and network with several businesses in the event and wedding industry. Though life served various curve balls, it was Dr. Myla's faith, passion, and perseverance that molded her into the woman she is today. Her philosophy is "If you want to touch the future, then you must teach, encourage and support our leaders of tomorrow."

Share what you do and your experience with education.

As an educator, I've been in the school system for 17 years. I started my career as a second-grade teacher and had the opportunity to work in various grade levels. My experience in education started off at a high climax, where I wanted to take part in any and everything, from being a classroom teacher to being a dance and step coach, to holding office in the Parent Teacher Association, and to working as a tutor in the afterschool program. I wanted to do more. I wanted to be a change agent in education, so I pursued the idea of being an instructional curriculum coach where I could help scholars school-wide.

As an instructional curriculum coach, I had the pleasure of not only supporting twenty scholars in a classroom but now supporting an entire school. Friends and family thought I had lost it when I decided to leave a school that was known to have a history of passing grades and now go to a low-performing school. I accepted the challenge! I had to step out of my comfort zone with the understanding that there would be times of being uncomfortable if I wanted to grow in my profession. With that being said, I am proud to say the school improved. That chapter of my education experience lasted for a year before moving on to a district position. My hunger to do more needed to be fed. Unfortunately, with the additional changes happening throughout the school year and schools facing being closed or re-purposed, I positioned myself to seek other opportunities. Currently, I am an instructional specialist supporting schools district-wide, where I now understand the greater impact and how education can be impacted when we don't change our mindset.

What is one thing you love the most about being a teacher, or if you are no longer teaching, what do you love most about your new profession?

Well, one thing I love the most about being a teacher is being around children. I've always been passionate about loving and caring and being a mentor to children. I started off as a Sunday school teacher, and it was always embedded in me that one day, little miss Natasha would be a great teacher. I look forward to seeing a child who once was shy and struggling and now outspoken and proficient in their academics. Students come to me like a blank canvas, and as their teacher, I have the opportunity to help paint a masterpiece. What I love about being an educator is being intentional in pouring positivity and self-love into each child.

As a teacher, I love seeing the smiles on my students' faces, the importance of student-teacher relationships, and the love of coming to school wanting to learn. I love being their cheerleader because there are times some students may not get that at home. It is my goal to ensure that I keep them engaged and knowing that, as their teacher, I am there for them. Just know that I am their advocate, and when they walk through the building and enter my classroom doors, they are loved and know that their teacher cares.

Therefore, being a teacher comes with numerous perks, but the greatest of them all is being a motivator and, most importantly, their coach. So that is why I love being a teacher.

What are some challenges you've faced as a teacher?

There are a few challenges that I've faced as a teacher, and those challenges sometimes come from *not getting the support that you may need from administration* and *not always getting the support that you may need from some of your parents*. For example, there are times some parents may think that when the children come to school, it's 100% up to the teacher when in reality, it's a team effort. I remind those parents that it's a team and community effort. Now, I do have parents that support me, but you have parents that say, hey, it's all you; you're the teacher. So sometimes it can be a bit challenging, especially if that child doesn't attend any classes, if that child missed an excessive amount of days from school, and if that child doesn't come with supplies. So just ensuring that you have someone at the school to support.

Another challenge that I face as a teacher is scenarios where *unrealistic expectations are set by the "People of Power."* There are some educational decisions that are made by people who have never been in a classroom to understand the realistic point of view of a teacher and expect teachers to "make it work." I'm a true advocate. If you want to see improvements in education, let's call the people who are in the trenches to the table to brainstorm, collaborate and execute a plan. It's about the buy-in! We're teachers, and of course, our job is to teach, but sometimes the "People of Power" think that teachers can turn water into wine, and at times it's hard to execute those expectations if teachers don't have the proper resources to deliver.

Teacher Salary is another challenge. As a teacher, there are times that we have to spend money to purchase items in order for a highly-engaged lesson to be executed with fidelity. Treats and prizes need to be purchased in order to motivate students. With inflation, items have increased, and so should teacher salaries. As a teacher, I will do my best to ensure that the students have what they need. Challenges occur when you don't have the support of the people who all play a role in ensuring teachers are equipped, motivated, and prepared for the success of a student.

If you could give two tips to a new teacher reading this book, what would they be?

Two tips that I would give to a new teacher reading this book. Tip 1: *Come into this profession with an open mind knowing that you will make a difference.* Tip 2: *Never stop loving your students.* Please keep in mind that these tips come from 17 years of experience and are helpful to beginning teachers. When a new teacher comes into this profession with an open mind, they must be ready to impart their pearls of wisdom and allow opportunities to learn from other teachers. This can range from learning effective strategies and best practices to the ins and outs of being a new educator.

Never stop loving your students. Students will come to school ready to deliver when they know and feel that their teacher cares for them. As a beginning teacher, it's important to build a relationship with your students. Yes, we may come to work not in the best of moods, but when those babies walk through our classroom doors, they look forward to having a great day. Now, there may be times a student may come in not engaged and is having a bad day. Let's be that change agent, peel back the onion, find ways to shift their demeanor, and keep them engaged and back on track. It's all about being creative! A former Principal of mine once said, "a teacher with-it-ness will take them far." A student will go that extra mile for any teacher they have a positive relationship with. Always remember, not only are we teachers, but we are also coaches, mentors, counselors, guardians, and an advocate. Make a difference, and never stop loving your students.

If you stayed in the classroom, what motivated you to stay, and what advice would you provide to someone who was in a similar position? Or if you left the classroom, what influenced that decision, and how did you decide your next steps?

Well, I'm currently working outside the classroom. What motivated me to stay and work outside the classroom was flexible opportunities to support both teachers and students and provide professional development and make a greater impact in numerous schools. The advice that I would give someone that is in a similar position is to remain focused, keep away from the negativity, and always document what support was provided. Put everything in black and white by keeping track of a specific school's growth or student's achievement. There will be times politics and other outside noise will stand in the way but learn how to curb them all and do what's needed to be done. Some may say that being a teacher is "easy," but do understand that this profession is not for everyone. You need patience, creativity, passion, love for children, and being equipped to deliver various lessons, all while keeping a rapport with parents and community members. If you're still in the classroom, then a teacher must keep a relationship with 20 different families minimum.

I've had my years of experience in the classroom. I've had the chance to build relationships with teachers, administration, parents, and, most importantly, students. I couldn't have done it all if I wasn't intentional with relationship building. Connect with students before the curriculum. Being too task-oriented can make or break a relationship between two individuals. Get to know how someone is doing before diving straight into work.

I advise you not to come into this position to prove a point but to come into this position to make a difference and a greater impact. Every student would want to excel in their achievement.

At the end of the day, a student will constantly ask, did I make you proud? Did I pass my assessment? What can I do to improve? And what can I do to be a better student in the classroom? So my advice for anyone that would like to be a teacher, though teachers are underpaid, is if you have a passion for teaching students and making a difference, then it will never be work if you love what you do. Most importantly, always remember, *a scholar will come to school ready to work as long as you, the teacher, build a relationship with them and reassure them that you are there for them every step of the way.*

And what motivated you to stay?

What motivated me to stay in my current position is the children. Working outside the classroom, you are mainly focusing more on adult learning. When having the opportunity to work with students, co-teach a lesson, or model an activity at the end of the lesson, a student will blurb out, "Dr. Myla, I wish you were my teacher and wish that you could stay a little longer." It reminds me of the many students I've made a great impact on in the past and are now educators, nurses, police officers, or business owners. It's always the students for me.

If I'm out having dinner with family and/or friends, more than likely, a former student will walk up to me, elated, and say, "Because of you, I attended this college. Because of you, I joined the same sorority. Because of you, I've started this career, and because of you, I am who I am today." So if I can continue to pour that same positive energy into every student I interact with, imagine how many other children I can make a difference with.

Why is a book like this needed?

A book like this is needed because it's a collaboration of educators who've experienced good and bad challenges and witnessed a shift in the field of education. The information in this book provides aspiring teachers to hear experiences from fellow educators and have an understanding of what is expected in the world of teaching. You will hear perspectives from various former and current educators across the United States based on their real-life experiences. Consider this book a wealth of knowledge that can assist beginning teachers and put the profession of teaching into a whole new light.

This is the raw and uncut of teaching. This is to teach or not to teach. Our intention is to provide hope to all aspiring, beginning, current, or former teachers with insights into the different walks of life of educators. It is intended to educate and motivate. Not only is this book needed for educators, but it is also needed for anyone who is in a profession and learning ways to make an impact in their field.

Based on your experience, what would you say to a teacher who is unsure about whether to stay or leave the classroom?

Based on my experience, I would have a discussion with the teacher to dive into their true feelings and thoughts and ask themselves, "How would you feel if you stayed in the classroom or if you were to leave the classroom?" Are you still passionate about teaching? Many educators are still in the classroom and are no longer happy, which causes more of a deficit for the students. Think about if you're still making a positive impact on your students. Now, don't get me wrong, teachers may have the desire to teach but are not happy with how the field may have changed based on politics, low salary pay, toxic work environment, in search of change, and so much more.

Take the time to reflect and ask yourself, is my heart all in, or have I had a change of heart? At the end of the day, this decision is up to the teacher. What I would say is think about it, pray on it, reflect, and if anything, take a piece of paper, write the pros, write the cons, and see how your thoughts are aligned. Because at the end of the day, I would want that teacher to be truly happy based on the decision they made versus someone else's decision.

If you had the power to change something in the education system, what would it be and why?

Now, this is one of my favorite questions. If I had the power to change something in the education system, it would be *teacher salaries*. Teachers work extremely hard. Teachers bring work home. Teachers work on the weekend. Granted, many people say that, well, we have summers off, we have holidays. But teachers are with those students more than they are with their own parents. So if a teacher comes in and gives their all 110%, let the paycheck show. There are other professions that make an overwhelming amount of money, and teachers get the bare minimum.

Teachers are constantly taking money out of their pockets to ensure that the student who was not able to pay for that field trip can attend, the student without lunch money can eat, and the student who is constantly improving can get awarded. If a student comes into a classroom with no school supplies, a teacher will spend their hard-earned money to ensure they are equipped to be successful. So why not look out for our teachers? Why not show appreciation to our educators financially? The cost of living has increased, the price of food has increased, and inflation has risen, so if everything is going up, why not increase teacher salaries?

Doctors, nurses, attorneys, and lawyers were all taught by teachers. It's because of a teacher many are successful today. A wise woman once said, "A good education can change anyone, but a good teacher can change EVERYTHING."

Acknowledgments

Dieudonne Cherubin
TIFFANY Davis
Schqueena Hill, @simply_que, www.nklusivekloset.com
Watson Louidor
Milius Myla
Milius Myla
Marie Rho
Jamillah Shakir, @JamTheBox
Monica Stokes

Delisha Easley

Instagram - iamdelishae
Facebook - DelishaE
Linkedin - delishaeasley
www.delishae.com

Delisha Easley is an international keynote speaker, leadership consultant, author, and inspiring educator. Delisha's message has spread globally, and has helped allow her audiences to identify and flourish in their purpose. Life experience has provided her with the expertise to develop effective strategies to reach people through exceptional methods. Her impact on social media, top-tier speaking engagements, and series of best-selling books have aided Delisha in the development of a multitude of life learners.

Professional organizations, school districts, and multiple corporations have implemented Delisha's strategies and methods, allowing them to take their business or classroom audiences to the next level; most importantly their personal life. When she is not involved in community-based initiatives, Delisha can be found almost anywhere across the globe, locked in with a game of chess, or engaged in a thrilling outdoor activity. Allow her the opportunity to share her expertise with you!

Share what you do and your experience with education.

I'm an Educational Consultant who speaks and trains educational leaders. My current job is as a Product Manager at a tech company. My experience within education goes back to high school when I first started volunteering with a United Way literacy program at the local elementary school. The program asked high school seniors to take an elective to go read with the elementary students.

I had a genuine passion for the classroom and for teaching; seeing children learn and finding unique ways to help them learn was great. That volunteer experience led me to go to college and major in Special Education with a minor in Teaching English as a Second Language. After completing an internship in each major and graduating, I began my career as an elementary school teacher at a private school.

Two years later, I received my Master's in Psychology and started doing other things in education; becoming a Director was one of those. Around 2012 is when I started the consulting aspect in regard to helping other people with their schools and outlining what works best, how to start if it's a private school, and how to start individual growth and professional development. Professional development in the classroom, with the administration team, and with the staff. Later I became an International teacher in Venezuela, and between working, I also coached sports and was an ESL tutor.

Therefore, my holistic perspective on education is truly based on my over ten years of experience in the educational system in private, public, and international schools.

What is one thing you love the most about being a teacher, or if you are no longer teaching, what do you love most about your new profession?

What I love the most about teaching is the direct impact that you have on the upcoming generation. Teachers are so influential, and the education system does not financially compensate them for all they do. Almost every person can credit some part of their life to either a teacher or a coach for a life-changing positive encounter. To have that responsibility is more than a career choice; it's a calling, and I would say that gift is just priceless.

Since I'm no longer in the day-to-day classroom in my new profession, I found that my teaching experience has helped me be a better manager of people. As well as seeing and helping people reach their career goals and helping their goals come to fruition, understanding how others work and knowing how to make that pivot if need be is a great skill to have, especially as a leader. I've seen these teaching skills help in communication as well. Knowing how someone learns or retains information lets you know if you were really "heard" in a training. For example, some people are visual learners, hands-on, and auditory. To present the best material is to include all of these learning styles. Teachers, in-person or virtual, are making an exciting experience yet educational experience for their students because they care. My experience as a teacher has definitely infiltrated my current career in tech.

What are some challenges you've faced as a teacher?

One of the main challenges I remember is not having good mentors or not having access to good mentors. Meaning, that your school may assign a mentor to you, and it's usually a person who has seniority but not necessarily a passion to continue to work in the field or even have a love still for the field. So you get kind of this advice and not a practical application or is given in a negative aspect that nothing will work. Those challenges, unfortunately, are more common than not, and also why many are leaving the field.

Other challenges were limited resources and having to be very creative about where you're going to get your lesson plan materials, always a shortage of supplies and funds to get more. And in special education, you need certain tools sometimes for certain students to even understand the work. Being creative on how to build weighted vests was something I didn't learn in college but had to figure out for my students to get what they needed from my classroom. Having creative ways to handle situations because you can't really just call administrators because the Special Education classroom was the students' last option. Another challenge that many teachers face is not getting paid enough. The recognition that you receive is good, but a lot of times, money is needed. The final challenge, I would say, is finances. It's hard as a caring teacher to financially live on your income, with a family especially, and provide what your classroom needs.

If you could give two tips to a new teacher reading this book, what would they be?

Let me try to keep this to two. Stay the course, there's a purpose in the process, and never stop teaching, even if you leave the classroom.

If you stayed in the classroom, what motivated you to stay, and what advice would you provide to someone who was in a similar position? Or if you left the classroom, what influenced that decision, and how did you decide your next steps?

Yes, my influence of leaving the classroom is that I knew going into education that my role as a teacher was only for a season of my life. My calling was broader than the classroom. I don't want to say greater. I just want to say broader because the classroom is still a great place for an Educator to be in.

My next steps were praying and asking God for direction and getting really clear and strategic on what that was going to look like, and understanding that the foundations of a teacher and what you gain as an educator literally can go into any profession after that.

So then my next plan was, what else was I passionate about? And it was technology and what does that look like from a nontech perspective? And that's how I made my Pivot into my current profession.

Why is a book like this needed?

I believe this book is needed to encourage those who are in the classroom and those who are thinking about leaving the classroom. This book, I think, through our stories, will help others get clarity on where they really are and where they need to be, and understanding where they came from is just a building block, if you will, to whatever they're destined to do. And then I think also it will light a fire in those who are teaching to continue to teach and kind of find their first love again, if you will, and be encouraged to stay the course and keep moving forward and impacting the generation.

Based on your experience, what would you say to a teacher who is unsure about whether to stay or leave the classroom?

If you are unsure about whether to stay or leave, ask yourself, is this aligned with my ultimate calling, her destiny? Don't be weary of purpose. We all get tired, we get irritated, and sometimes just angry at the overall education system. But if you still feel the responsibility to stay, then I would say stay. The same applies to leaving. Don't leave the classroom to chase money, because you will never be fulfilled. We all need to reaffirm. We are where we need to be. I can recall when I was in Venezuela and had a very bad experience with the whole hostage situation and getting robbed and stuff.

I had a decision to make to either leave the country or finish the school year because this happened in February. And my compassion for the students and love for teaching caused me to make a decision, which was tough, to stay in the country until the end of the school year in June. And so I was very grateful for that. I did have a support system to help me through that process, but I knew that my calling outweighed that one experience, so I stayed.

If you had the power to change something in the education system, what would it be and why?

I would change a few things.

One would be *funding to schools,* obviously increasing teachers' salaries. And when I say funding to schools, the breakdown of how funding is split to schools, lower some administrators' salaries, or just make them a base salary across the board. And, of course, demolish the education jail pipeline that's been plaguing our nation for decades.

I won't go on a tangent about that, but you can research that yourself. As a former special education teacher, I could see early on how quickly they want to label students, and then that label follows the student. Unfortunately, and in a lot of cases, defines them as a person, which is not accurate.

Even if the student was mislabeled, they have a difficult time moving forward throughout their educational path. So *having various ways of educating students*, I think we'll have fewer diagnoses. It used to be you waited till children were about eight years old in the third grade to do some of the tests that they are now conducting as early as preschool because you were giving the child an opportunity to develop.

Certain things that people did, maybe in kindergarten, they end up just naturally stopped doing by the time they got to the third grade.

I think things like that give space and opportunity. My personal story, I probably would have been labeled being on the borderline of Asperger's or Autism because I didn't talk till I was three years old. My parents said I just stated a sentence one day.

The last thing will be, especially in America, *diagnosing things with pills.* We are getting children addicted to some type of drug early on to where they feel that this is the only way they can function. I had an experience with a student in a Special Ed class who had numerous pills that he was taking, and he knew that these pills helped him calm down. So he really wanted to go on a field trip, and we caught him in the hallway, trying to take three or four; he was only eight years old. Thank God we caught him, and he wasn't able to swallow them.

In his mind, he just knew that this was going to help me so that he could go on a field trip, not understanding the implications of his help. Teachers, we need you in the classroom, and when you leave, please remain a lifetime advocate.

Kimberly Simons

Instagram - kimberlythepurposecoach
Facebook - purposefirst
Linkedin - kimberlythepurposecoach
www.thysisterskeeper.org

Kimberly Simons, "The Purpose Coach," is a long-time resident of a suburb outside of Atlanta, Georgia. She has been a non-fiction writer since childhood, when she first began writing poetry while growing up in Cincinnati, Ohio. Despite her love of writing, she is only now making her debut as a published author. She has spent most of her life in Education. However, her voracious appetite for reading and learning has proven Personal Development as her primary interest while she strives always to be a little better than she was the day before. As a certified Women's Empowerment and Life Coach, her experience with mindset and transformation, combined with her intuitive nature, make her an influential speaker. She believes wholeheartedly that women are much more alike than they are different, and those similarities should be the ties that bond women everywhere.

Kim founded Thy Sister's Keeper in 2019 as an organization that would stand in support and encouragement of women becoming connected and empowered globally. Within Sister's Keeper, LLC, Kim helps women move beyond the secrets that have kept them from living happy lives to step up to a new level of empowerment as they walk in the purpose and joy they've always dreamed possible. Through group and one-on-one guided coaching sessions, she teaches from her proprietary "Purpose First" coaching program framework, which helps women heal from previous limiting beliefs and re-create their new, more confident identities. Kim is planning the release of four books before the end of 2022. When she is not stealing one more moment of writing time, she enjoys family movies with her husband, Jeff, and their two beautiful daughters, Sydney and

Teagan. To learn more about Kimberly, follow her on SM or seek www.ThySistersKeeper.org.

Share what you do and your experience with education.

I currently am working as a Talent and Gifted (TAG) lead teacher for middle school, and in that role, I work on differentiating the lessons that the students receive so that we're teaching strategies to meet their different learning styles. We're accelerating their actual learning.

However, there may be some areas where they're a little weaker than others because TAG students are sometimes stronger in some areas than others. So we'll still focus on those areas where they may need a little more help. However, I have been teaching, for this is going into my 26th year of teaching.

Prior to the TAG role, I taught elementary, mostly math and science.

What is one thing you love the most about being a teacher, or if you are no longer teaching, what do you love most about your new profession?

The thing that I love the most about being a teacher is the relationships that I establish with the students and the parents. I absolutely love knowing that I have a positive influence on how they feel about the world and how they view learning. I feel that it's very important that they learn, at an early age, how to see the world in a positive way and establish within themselves the visions that they have for their lives and the visions that they have for an ideal world.

What are some challenges you've faced as a teacher?

Teaching involves many challenges. I think anyone would agree. One challenge is *that you're dealing with the children and families from so many diverse backgrounds representing many different ways of thinking and many different ways of doing things. Sometimes there's a clash of personalities and behaviors as a result of those differences. Oftentimes the clash is between home or family norms versus school rules and expectations. It can be very difficult to find a common ground.*

So the various family dynamics that impact how students socialize or how they behave in the classroom, even the priority or the importance that families place on education and the student's potential for future goals or future accomplishments, can potentially wreak havoc in the classroom.

If you could give two tips to a new teacher reading this book, what would they be?

The number one piece of advice is *to go into each school year with the plan and the intention of building relationships with the parents.* If you put in the effort to establish positive and open communication with the parents with which you are in frequent communication, you establish a trust that can carry you through the school year and beyond. Parents just want to know that you've accepted that position for the right reasons, that you will care about their child while they are in your care, and that you are ultimately on the side of the child. It really makes a huge difference because if you can establish parents as allies, you reduce behavior issues, you gain support from home, and you establish a connection of respect and cooperation with your students that will make a huge difference in the success of your school year.

The second thing would be *staying focused on your why*. Because things are going to get tough, and you need to be able to fall back on your reason for going into education in the first place.

If you stayed in the classroom, what motivated you to stay, and what advice would you provide to someone who was in a similar position? Or if you left the classroom, what influenced that decision, and how did you decide your next steps?

Actually, I took half a school year off this past year because last year was "a lot!" Returning to full face-to-face teaching turned out to be more challenging than we anticipated. Along with everything that was happening in school, I was having some challenges that were going on personally with the health of my family. And so, I did find a need to step out for the second half of the school year.

In deciding to go back, I really felt led because I had a purpose for going into teaching in the first place, and I realized I had not fulfilled that purpose yet. I still needed to make myself available for the children, to just do my part for future generations, letting them know that they're capable of anything that they put their minds to, just continuing to encourage them to go after their dreams.

Why is a book like this needed?

A book like this has a critical need if you're considering going into a field like teaching. You need to know all of it, and I want to say the secrets behind it, the things that people may not share. Because so often, teaching is like a brochure. They're giving you the positive, but you need to know the good, the bad, and the ugly because once you're in it, you're in it, and you need to be properly prepared so that you can do the best job that you can, as well as being able to take care of yourself emotionally, mentally, physically, all of the things that are going to prove to be worn out. Let's just be honest!

It's important that you go into any career with an understanding of what is involved and what is expected, but especially so in a job that involves relationships. If there's any chance that you are not equipped with the proper patience, you can actually do more harm than good. Many students during the pandemic have really been seeking a soft place to land. If you can't say for sure that you fit that description, please do not apply.

Based on your experience, what would you say to a teacher who is unsure about whether to stay or leave the classroom?

If you're trying to decide whether to stay or leave education, it requires you to take time to really reflect on whether you are capable of meeting the needs of the students, the families, your teaching team, and your school. However, you also have to decide whether your needs are being met. Consider whether you are receiving a sufficient level of support to meet school expectations. Ask yourself if it has just become a job or do you still enjoy what you do. Consider your level of wellness in the areas of emotional, physical, and mental health. Teaching is more than a notion. So leaving teaching should also require thought. You need to sit with the idea. You need to really think about the blessings that come from teaching as well as the challenges.

If you had the power to change something in the education system, what would it be and why?

The first thing I would want to change in the education system is a greater focus on social and emotional learning. We have turned our focus so much toward testing that I feel like we're not focusing on how the world is changing. As the world changes and we're failing to prepare our children for those changes, we're really leaving them unprepared to successfully be self-sufficient contributors as they approach the age at which they will need to be capable of navigating the world. Instead, studies are reporting an increase in depression, childhood suicides, and mental health issues. Incorporating more social-emotional learning would help in addressing these numbers.

For teachers who are consistently addressing these needs in the schools, there should be an increase in teachers' pay. There needs to be recognition, value, and respect for what teachers do. Nobody goes into teaching for the money or recognition. However, wouldn't it be nice to be acknowledged?

Brittney Bolden

Instagram - a_teacher_like_me

Owner of A Teacher Like Me graduated from The University of West Alabama with a BS in Mathematics and a Master of Arts in Teaching in Mathematics. I have worked in education for eight years. I have taught 7th grade, 8th grade, pre-algebra, Algebra 1, and geometry. I reside in Tuscaloosa, Alabama, with my daughter Rhyian. Teaching is my passion. I honestly believe it is a calling.

Share what you do and your experience with education.

I am a current 8th-grade middle school math teacher in Tuscaloosa, Alabama. I just recently entered my 9th year of teaching. I have taught in three different school districts, having worked in four different schools in total. My experience with education has been quite the roller coaster ride, but I still managed to stay the course. I have experienced highs and lows along this nine-year journey, but I truly believe it is my calling. Education is definitely where I am supposed to be. Despite considering changing careers in the past, something always led me to stay another year. Now, look at me nine years later.

What is one thing you love the most about being a teacher, or if you are no longer teaching, what do you love most about your new profession?

One thing I love the most about being a teacher is seeing the underdog rise to the occasion. Don't get me wrong, I believe academic scholars who maintain honor roll should be celebrated, but so do the students that honestly try their hardest, and the outcome is a "C." I know for a fact when you are at the bottom, the only other place to go is up! With that being said, I love to see students rise to their personal goals, making not only their parents and family proud but their teachers proud as well.

What are some challenges you've faced as a teacher?

This is a question that I had a difficult time answering, but I narrowed it down to four major things. The first challenge is having a full-time career but still struggling to make ends meet. It is tough being a single parent having to work two jobs just to maintain. I, as well as several of my fellow colleagues, have a second job just to support ourselves and our families. I had to start my own business named "A Teacher Like Me, LLC" just to ensure that my daughter and I had all that we needed until the next pay period. All that we go through and do as an educator, you would think we would get paid a wage that can support ourselves and our families.

Another challenge is finding the energy to come home to parent my own daughter after giving all of my energy to someone else's child all day. Before I had my daughter, I would ride home in silence or get home and just have quiet time because I spent eight to ten hours talking all day. That daily routine had to change because I found that it was a disadvantage for my own daughter. I found myself talking less with my child as soon as I got home because I was exhausted from talking all day. I quickly had to adjust and find a balance because she deserves me the most out of any child.

The third challenge is being able to complete the demands and deadlines given but also teach my students the standards necessary to be successful on the state exams.

And then the last thing is finding an administrative team who supports the whole teacher and the whole child equally and respectively. Often we get held to a standard that our students and parents are not held to, and it is frustrating. Some may even call it unfair. I can gladly say in the new school I am in, I do have an administrative team where the staff is not invisible as well as the students. It took me seven years to find such a team, but I am thankful to have done so. Better late than never, right?

If you could give two tips to a new teacher reading this book, what would they be?

One of the first things is to *set clear boundaries as it relates to your personal life and professional life.* Try your best to keep the two separate as much as possible. In my nine-year journey, the very first mentor I had told me something very simple but oh-so powerful. She told me to "never bring my work home with me." She said to use my planning period to do what I can and what I can't do, try again tomorrow.

The second thing is to remember your mental health is the most important. If you aren't able to show up for yourself every day, there is no way you can show up and be there for your students, your family, your spouse, or your children. Always remember it is ok to take some time out for yourself. You'll be glad you did!

If you stayed in the classroom, what motivated you to stay, and what advice would you provide to someone who was in a similar position? Or if you left the classroom, what influenced that decision, and how did you decide your next steps?

I stayed because, first, I was too invested as far as retirement goes before I started to have a change of heart. Most importantly, I stayed because I have bigger dreams within the educational field, and I know that the classroom is not my final destination. I wanted to pursue the task of becoming either a math coach or even working in higher education, and those are just two of my short-term goals. My biggest goal is to be an entrepreneur and have my own math tutoring center. I know that my journey in education will not end here, so I am just gaining experience. When I make it to my final destination in my educational career, I want to be the very best educator I can be.

If I could provide any advice to someone who is in a similar position, I would say to dream big. The sky isn't the limit when people have walked on the moon! Do not get complacent when there is greatness lying within.

Why is a book like this needed?

Everyone, no matter the field or profession, has sat under the sound of a teacher's voice. Although the profession is overlooked, our voices still deserve to be heard. The best doctors, the best lawyers, the best nurses, and even the best teachers have been taught by an educator. The good, the bad, and the ugly truth that many try to suppress as it pertains to education will be discussed throughout this book. I believe that it is past time for our voices to be heard, and this book is the perfect way to do it.

Based on your experience, what would you say to a teacher who is unsure about whether to stay or leave the classroom?

I would advise them to carefully weigh their options and not make a life-altering decision when their emotions are running rampant. Just take some time, and think things through thoroughly. Remember, everything isn't for everyone, so it is okay to reevaluate your career options. One thing I know personally is if it is meant for you to stay in education, you will always come back to it. The most important advice I have is if you believe in prayer, pause, pray to our most high God, and ask for your steps to be ordered, for I believe that God will see you through and direct your path in the direction that is best for you.

If you had the power to change something in the education system, what would it be and why?

I believe the biggest thing will probably be accountability or the accountability level for the students and their parents. It will have to match the pressure and accountability that is placed on us as teachers. When certain states were required to take state exams in order to be promoted to the next grade and/or graduate, students took school much more seriously. Once those accountability pieces were removed, the main goal of success seemed to have shifted.

We, as teachers, are here to fulfill our contract beyond the call of duty. We work hour after hour on and off the clock. We coach or sponsor sports and extracurricular activities, we go to sporting events, we are placed on committees that hold additional responsibilities, then we come home to grade papers because our planning periods were taken up with meetings or calling parents. I feel that students and parents should be able to fulfill a contract as well because I know that we, the teacher, the parents, and the students, all have a job to do. It takes everyone to do their part in order for everyone to be successful and for everyone to accomplish the specific goals at hand.

Acknowledgments

LaTonia Brown-Edwards, www.eaabs.com
Karla James
Marie Bender, @Marie_elizabeth_hair, Marieelizabethhair.com
Celester & Teressa Bolden Jr., @22loves44
J C Booker
Tandra Dixon,
Dequisha Epps, @Shebeauti, www.shebeauti.net
ShaDonna Johnson
MAKAYLA MOFFETT, @ladiicamil
Angela Parham
Kanesha Pryor

Monica Tookes

Instagram - tookestimeteach
Facebook - tookestime
www.tookestime.com

Monica Tookes is a Certified Educator, Entrepreneur, Author, Empowering Speaker, and a Purpose Coach. She officially started her journey as a teacher in 2018 and is passionate about instructing students and adults while fostering lifelong learners. She believes in ACTIVATING her God-given purpose while encouraging and empowering others to do the same.

Share what you do and your experience with education.

I previously taught second and third grade for three years, and I have a master's degree in educational leadership. Now, I am a full-time entrepreneur and work as a freelance educational consultant. I've held the position of Director of Operations for a company that hosts after-school programs across the United States, teaching financial literacy. I also help teachers effectively use technology to enhance their lessons, differentiate instruction for diverse learners, and avoid the burden of burnout. Lastly, I have a tutoring company that focuses on promoting academic achievement by fostering lifelong learners.

What is one thing you love the most about being a teacher, or if you are no longer teaching, what do you love most about your new profession?

I love that teaching is not limited to the four walls of a classroom. As a business owner, I can confidently say that you can teach in whatever setting is conducive for you. I have the privilege of teaching children and adults. In fact, I saw a need that was not being fulfilled in many schools. I found that teachers are burned out, students are not engaged in learning, and student performance data revealed that learning was regressing or remained stagnant. I decided to leave the classroom and pursue a new career in educational consulting. This allows me to teach educators how to enhance their instruction, help close the achievement gap, and continue doing what I love.

What are some challenges you've faced as a teacher?

One challenge that I faced as a teacher was the extensive certification tests. As a matter of fact, I had to take the Elementary Education Florida Teacher Certification Test (FTCE) six times in order to pass, and even after passing, I was still told that that wasn't enough. After becoming a certified educator, I saw that many teachers were considered out of field because they did not have the new reading or ESOL endorsements. This added to the stress level of teachers because it was another box to check off. The purpose of this mandate was to increase the number of certified educators in classrooms. However, it did the opposite when many overqualified teachers left the profession because they felt they were underappreciated and undervalued. This left many vacant classes that would either be divided into classrooms that were already at the peak of their capacity or be filled by a slew of uncertified teachers, creating a problem even greater than the original issue.

Another challenge that I faced was the lack of resources in my school. My Amazon purchase statement indicated that I spent an average of $200 a week on supplies, tools to enhance my lessons, curriculum, decorations, and so much more. I even had to purchase fans because the air conditioning unit at our school rarely worked. I thought this was an isolated issue, but after further research, many teachers faced the same challenge. I also had to purchase technology because our school was not privileged to have one-to-one devices. We were lucky to have three computers working in each classroom.

    I often wonder how I was able to fund my classroom and manage my living expenses. I sacrificed a lot to make sure my students had a valuable education. Some teachers have to pick up a second job to make ends meet. After taxes and my summer pay deduction, I rarely had enough money to pay all of my bills. A lot of people don't know that many teachers do not get paid for the summer, so they have to put part of their paycheck away, teach summer school, or work another job to have money over the break. That's definitely a challenge for many teachers.

    Lastly, teachers wear multiple hats. I've been the guidance counselor, the nurse, the chef, the janitor, the mentor, the entertainer, the event planner, the detective, and the coach. Because of that, the long hours and constant withdrawal affect our mental health. That's ultimately the main challenge that educators face, which is causing them to deal with the burden of burnout. I dedicated my life to teaching, and I lost myself in the process. The constant meetings, professional development, behavior management, data collection, making copies, decorating, parent-teacher conferences, lesson planning, evaluations, and grading papers left me burned out. I had no boundaries in place, and I had to step away from the classroom in order to identify what it was that I loved about teaching, so I could continue doing what I loved.

If you could give two tips to a new teacher reading this book, what would they be?

I would say *enforce boundaries*. I don't just say set them because it's one thing to say, I'm going to do something. It's another to actually enforce and do it. So what does that look like? Work your contracted hours. We must learn how to go home and rest, go for a walk, spend time with family, hang out with friends, or do anything other than work! So many teachers work overtime when their brains are already on overload. I know there is a lot of work to do, but that work will still be there the next day. The thing about a teacher's job, it never ends. So you have to set and *enforce* those boundaries so you don't overwhelm yourself and become burned out. Another part of enforcing boundaries is taking your lunch break and avoiding the toxic teacher's lounge. Make sure that you're taking nonnegotiable breaks so you can regroup, refocus and reset. If not, it is impossible to be an effective educator. Take time to fill up your cup so you actually have something to pour into your students.

The second tip that I would give is to *advocate for yourself*. Learn to say no. I know that may sound combative, but really it's not. If you are asked to do something and you do not feel mentally, physically, or professionally up to it, it's okay to say no. You could also try saying, I don't have the bandwidth for that task at this time. And that's totally okay. If you constantly accept tasks without taking inventory of your bandwidth, you will become burned out. Advocating for yourself also entails asking for support. Teachers receive a lot of mandates, and many of us are so passionate about the profession that we defy our limits and take on a "make it happen" mentality. That mindset also leads to burnout and forces us to sacrifice our sanity. You don't have to abide by unrealistic expectations. If you have too many students in your classroom, request a paraprofessional. If you need assistance with collecting, organizing, and/or analyzing data, you could ask for a coach to help you. If you are spending too much money on your classroom, look for donors or ask the administrative team for possible solutions. Remember, you are not in this alone. Advocate for yourself by seeking the support that you need and deserve.

If you stayed in the classroom, what motivated you to stay, and what advice would you provide to someone who was in a similar position? Or if you left the classroom, what influenced that decision, and how did you decide your next steps?

I left the classroom because I reached my capacity in that specific setting. I had to identify the capacity in which I was called to teach, and teaching second and third graders was limited to three years for me. During my final year in the classroom, I spent more time working with other teachers, facilitating workshops, and pouring into the student body than I did teaching in my classroom. At this point, I knew I was led to administration and desired to be a change agent for teachers and students.

It's very important that educators understand that you're not limited to one setting or one form of teaching. So, identifying what works best for you is essential. That's why I went and pursued my master's degree in Educational Leadership, and I transitioned from primarily teaching students to now teaching students and adults. I followed my passion, I'm fulfilled, and I am still teaching! So, that's how I was able to make my decision to leave and determine my next steps. I may have left the classroom, but I never left teaching.

Why is a book like this needed?

Many valuable educators are contemplating leaving the educational field, or they've already left. I believe that this book will really help teachers continue doing what they love in the capacity in which they're called to teach. I want educators to understand what teaching simply means. It's to share or to show or explain how to do something. We can do that in any environment. This book is going to help teachers hear from other educators, hear various perspectives, and understand that they're not alone in this walk. I want teachers to know that you can continue to do what you love without giving up on your passion or peace in the process.

Based on your experience, what would you say to a teacher who is unsure about whether to stay or leave the classroom?

Well, first and foremost, I would say rediscover your why.

Why do you want to become a teacher?

- *Did you want to see students succeed?*
- *Did you want to foster lifelong learners?*
- *Did you want to build relationships with students?*
- *Did you want to combat the myth that students can't learn?*

When you rediscover your why, don't give up on it! That's the first thing that I would say to a teacher who's unsure about staying or leaving. Also, don't allow burnout to turn you away from the profession or your passion. You chose to teach for a reason, so don't give up on it that easily. If you decide to leave the classroom, understand that your passion for teaching will never leave you. So identify where you need to go or what it is that you need to do to still fulfill your passion for educating others. This is not restricted to a classroom setting.

Lastly, identify the capacity in which you're called to teach. Maybe you want to become an administrator, instructional coach, professional development facilitator, educational consultant, tutor, start your own school, develop curriculum, or be on the school board. The options are endless, so do not give up on teaching. God gave you the gift, so continue to use it!

If you had the power to change something in the education system, what would it be and why?

I would change the educational system by starting with policy. I would make it mandatory for all politicians in the educational system to have at least three-plus years of teaching experience in a core subject class. I believe it takes educators to reform education. I would rally for this change because it would lead to educators' voices being valued and heard, higher salaries, less telling what to do and more demonstrating, higher student achievement, and more educators entering and staying in the profession.

Too many politicians hold positions of power without professional or practical experience teaching in a classroom. Resulting in the educational system being run like a shabby business lacking ethics and equity. We need to have more policymakers and politicians that have a background in teaching in a classroom so they can make the best decisions for the educational system as a whole. The current system is failing our students because it continues to fail our teachers. So, I do believe that having more teachers as educational leaders would lead to reform, and it would definitely help with the burnout that many teachers are currently facing.

Acknowledgments

Janay Blakely, @janay_blakely, www.ThePoetCo.com
Aliyah Bufford, @liabufford
R Franklin, @Renxjr
Hannah Gallina, @hannahpgallina
Samantha Laguerre, @Beingsamtv, Beingonepodcast.com
Janea Ruiz, @jhope19, RuizRegime.com
Arnecia Watson, @axbxw1, www.watsontutoringco.com
Mary Williams-Ervin
Leona White, @iworkout2

Stephanie Sanders

Instagram - stephaniejanay
Facebook - sjsanders4
Linkedin - stephaniejsanders4
www.stephaniejsanders.net

Stephanie Sanders is the founder and CEO of Cultivated Mind and Enterprises, where they inspire, educate, and cultivate you to be the person that you never had. She is also a High School English Educator of ten-plus years in the charter school sector, Teacher of the Year, and Teacher of Distinction by the National Society of High School Scholars and a proud member of Sigma Gamma Rho Sorority Incorporated.

Share what you do and your experience with education.

I've taught English eight through twelve grades, AP, Research, and Personal Finance. I've been the 504 coordinator, MTSS Coordinator 9-12, English Department Chair, and Cheerleading Coach of both JV and varsity (at the same time). I am currently the Tennis coach . I've taught honors-level English with core-level scholars in the same class, and I've been in leadership positions at various locations in charge of interviewing and giving criticism to new hires. I have been a mentor for many years.

Outside of my profession as an educator, I teach adults how to make money and build wealth for their families. I provide strategic and effective plans that provide stability for one's household. I am a financial educator and strategist.

What is one thing you love the most about being a teacher, or if you are no longer teaching, what do you love most about your new profession?

The scholars! Their personalities, and knowing that I'm making an impact on them every single day. Whether it's personally, educationally or as a coach. Because I do so many different things, I get to touch them in many different ways, and that's the best thing about what I do every day. I love being able to spark the minds of young adults. I love the fact that I can be the person I never had while growing up and share what I have learned. I am literally the change I want to see. I am just grateful that I get to inspire, cultivate and educate young minds on a daily basis.

What are some challenges you've faced as a teacher?

Well, as a teacher, there are many challenges I face. *I deal with administration, parents, and scholars on a daily basis. Some administrators are trying to dim your light, while others want you to grow. Some parents support your efforts, while some feel like I am a glorified babysitter. Some scholars have home training and some do not. It's you against each aspect, and the only people you have for support are your colleagues, who may or may not be trying to support you. It can be a lonely profession at times.*

Sometimes there's a difference in opinion as it concerns administration. They have a title, but no clue of the groundwork, so they tell you things that you know as an educator will not work for the population you serve. The people in charge sometimes lack morals, so what is commanded to do is not in the best interest of the scholar. As an educator, you want to be fair to all, but you risk losing your job. North Carolina does not protect teachers.

Another challenge would be *classroom management.* Your first year is always the hardest because you're just learning. But somewhere in my ten years, some classes, maybe like 1 or 2, have been a struggle, and doing that on your own without support from your administration makes it a lot harder. It mostly has to do with everybody that's not the scholars, always the outside forces. Let's be clear; the scholars are NOT the problem.

If you could give two tips to a new teacher reading this book, what would they be?

The first tip I would say is to *get a mentor and seek to be better*. Having someone that you work with that you can bounce ideas off of really helps. Have a mentor for the first three years and even the years after because it develops you as a teacher.

Two, be the change that you want to see. If teaching is your passion and you teach for a reason, like it wasn't, oh, I need money, so I'm going to be a teacher, and you really became a teacher to be a teacher, then be that change that you want to show your scholars. What you tell them, make sure you follow and that you live by what you tell them because they're watching. Always and literally Forever!

If you stayed in the classroom, what motivated you to stay, and what advice would you provide to someone who was in a similar position? Or if you left the classroom, what influenced that decision, and how did you decide your next steps?

Well, for me personally, going back to why I teach, for my scholars, I was that kid that didn't have a good home life, so school was my everything. I stayed at school as much as possible so I wouldn't stay home. Our profession is important. So there are some kids that don't eat, and there are some kids that don't have a roof. There are some kids that don't have heat. There are some that don't have pencils when they go home. There are some that have no guidance and are raising themselves, and some are raising younger siblings. Education steps up when home life can not in some cases.

So for me, what motivates me is knowing that any one of my scholars could be going through that, and I give them a place of protection, a positive environment in which they can grow. They can be successful regardless of what they go home to. I can only control my classroom. So the fact that I can control this environment and help scholars grow and think better of themselves, keeps me coming back every single day.

Why is a book like this needed?

Teachers need to hear from other educators that still have passion. In all honesty, this field is draining. It will suck the life from you if you let it. Educators need to know that it's not about how much you keep, it's about loving what you do and making a difference. Yes, we are underpaid and underappreciated, but WE MATTER, and WE ARE NEEDED and WE are Necessary. Money should not be the reason you leave the profession. You can turn your skill set into dollars outside of the classroom and still be an effective educator. You should ask me how. Keep your passion at the forefront. When you do something you love and have the funds to still do what you want, it does not get any better. I am here to tell you that it is possible.

Based on your experience, what would you say to a teacher who is unsure about whether to stay or leave the classroom?

When you wake up in the morning and your life is miserable and everything about what you got going on personally is bringing you down, and you go to work and you feel the same way, you need to get out of teaching. Leave the profession. But if you can go to work and those scholars still put a smile on your face regardless of whatever you have going on in your life, then STAY. That's a teacher we need.

If you had the power to change something in the education system, what would it be and why?

I would change *classes based on age and grades,* so my classes will be based on skill level regardless of age. Because you can have a 6th grader and he or she reads like a first grader, what does it matter if he or she is in the 6th grade if he or she can't read?

I would *eliminate classes by age* because everyone learns differently. I would change grades from numbers to proficient, not proficient and distinct, because numbers don't matter. As an educator, we know that numbers don't matter. No parent ever asks about a "good grade." Sometimes grades are there to appease. Whether a scholar gets a 90% or a 10% that doesn't always mean that he or she knows 90% or 10% of the material. It is just how well he or she did that day if he or she tried and in some cases grades are what they are because of outside pressures. I have had smart kids get low grades because they didn't like the school or the teacher. I would change these things in the system to give scholars a chance to feel empowered by the material and not driven by a number.

Too many parents and scholars are fixated on numbers and it leads to anxiety in the classroom, which affects learning. It causes high anxiety in scholars. There is too much emphasis on numbers that, in reality, are meaningless. It's the content that matters. I believe my suggestions will *empower our scholars instead of using these fixed societal norms to tear them down.*

Acknowledgments

Charlene Forrest, @Mscharleneforrest

Yolanda Dudley

Instagram - prettyinspiration08
Facebook - yolanda.dudley.779

Yolanda Dudley is a mother, wife, educator, and a certified school counselor at Oxford High School in Mississippi. She's been working with students across all grade levels for over 15 years. She received her bachelor's degree from Delta State University and her master's degree from the University of Southern Mississippi. After completing her bachelor's degree, she became a special education teacher. In 2011, she decided to pursue a school counseling degree. This degree would allow her to become a true change agent in her community; helping students become and be their absolute best in all areas. Yolanda has served as a certified school counselor in both Mississippi and California. She's had the opportunity to work with world-renowned counseling leaders and authors, helping to transform school counseling programs. Yolanda believes her best work is yet to come as she continues to pursue greatness as a change agent in the public school system.

Share what you do and your experience with education.

Currently, I am a high school counselor. I've been working in education for over 15 years. I have been a computer lab specialist, a parent liaison, and a special services teacher, and I'm now the school counselor. This is my eleventh year as a school counselor.

What is one thing you love the most about being a teacher, or if you are no longer teaching, what do you love most about your new profession?

The thing that I love the most about my new profession as a high school counselor is the opportunity to make an impression on young adults; to me, they are young adults.

High school students are learning to become young adults. This means that I get to contribute to their growth process. It's so awesome to watch them grow. It's amazing to sit down and have conversations with them just to see how intelligent they are and to see that they still need so much from us to grow. Being embedded in the school and community setting with these students is probably one of the best things about being a high school counselor.

What are some challenges you've faced as a teacher?

Some of the challenges that I faced as a teacher, especially as a special education teacher, were the variety of backgrounds of the students in my classroom. When I say backgrounds, I mean the level of learning and student cultural backgrounds. My first years as a special education teacher were in my hometown. I was born and raised in the community, making it easier for me to connect with them overall. The challenge was more so related to getting parent buy-in when it was time to manage behavior and talk about growth. Most of them saw me as the girl from the neighborhood and not a professional at first. Through hard work and a continuation of showing up in school and in the community, I gained knowledge to guide me and the respect and trust of my parents.

As a school counselor in the state of California, my challenges were more related to cultural issues. Not knowing as much about the Native American students or the Hispanic students seemed difficult at first. It was a challenge that made me grow.

If you could give two tips to a new teacher reading this book, what would they be?

The tip is to *Not give up*. Go through the process. Go through all the challenges. Allow them to contribute to your growth. When I was moved into the new position as a high school counselor, they asked me what I was most concerned about, and I told them that there wasn't really a concern about moving from middle school to high school. I kept an open mind and was eager to learn and grow forward. My statement to my supervisor was that "I would grow where I was planted." I've reminded myself of this statement every day on this journey. It has made difficult days easier and good days even brighter!

And so this is something that I find myself telling teachers, don't let an uncomfortable beginning deter you from the possible fulfilling ending.

The second tip is to make sure that you find *out as much as you can about your students*. Make sure you learn about who they are, where they come from, and where they are trying to go. Learn as much as you can about these students because, a lot of times, we make assumptions based on what we don't know.

If you stayed in the classroom, what motivated you to stay, and what advice would you provide to someone who was in a similar position? Or if you left the classroom, what influenced that decision, and how did you decide your next steps?

I left the classroom as a special education teacher. I did that for about four years, and I left the classroom. I just realized that wasn't the best area for me. I love what I do now. I love school counseling. It's something I've done my entire life. I knew that I could still continue to help children but in a different realm. The classroom setting was almost too enclosed for me.

There were lots of things that I could not do as a teacher that I could do as a counselor, and so that helped me to decide on what my next steps were going to be. Having an amazing counselor in my life as a high school student encouraged me to share the love. I knew that counseling was something that I was good at, and I wanted to do it.

Why is a book like this needed?

A book like this is needed because I talk to countless people every day that want to leave the classroom or that are thinking about leaving the classroom. The reality is that our children are still required to go to school every day. They're required to show up, and they need people to show up as well. They need teachers to show up and not just show up in the building but show up in the building overall. The people that are contemplating leaving the profession are some of the best! We need them!

Coming from a counselor's perspective and a counselor's heart, it's my intent to show kindness, to love these babies, and to be the change I want to see in the world. A book like this is needed because they need to see and hear both sides. There are both good and bad experiences, but they don't always have to end in not being in the classroom. There's a tremendous need for all children to have strong, reliable adults in their lives to truly get a whole school experience.

Based on your experience, what would you say to a teacher who is unsure about whether to stay or leave the classroom?

I would say to them that this is an experience; it's a journey. Don't base it on one thing that's happening in a classroom, one classroom setting, one class period, one class, and one student. It's an experience, and they should wholeheartedly go through that experience. Make sure their best effort is being put forth at all times. Find strategies and solutions. Don't base it solely on money and bad experiences. Do as much as you can, and at the end of the day, if that's not enough, then you do what you have to do.

If you had the power to change something in the education system, what would it be and why?

That's kind of a tough question. I would probably remove a lot of the stipulations and barriers that are put on teachers and on educators overall. There are so many barriers for teachers, counselors, and administrators to move beyond. There are a lot of logistical things that are hard to get around, and it makes it hard for us to truly do our job. Overall, I would change the way we provide services for our children. I would teach trauma-informed practices every chance that I got, and I would make sure that every educator was receiving the mental health care that they needed as well.

Acknowledgments

Tre Floyd, @Trefloydproductions, www.trefloyd.com
Victoria Hopkins, @torichenille
Earl Jones, @blakice24
LeTasha Jones, NA
Lisa Lairy, @empress_teelisa
Kjuana Moore-Curry, @roesqueencurry
Cynthia Pittman
Tina Gibson, @Tinakgibson1

Dr. Dashia Andrews

Instagram - dr.dashiaandrews
Facebook - drdashiaandrews
linkedin.com - drdashiaandrews
www.dashiaandrews.com

Dashia Andrews, Ph.D., is an educator, researcher, program developer, and non-profit executive with over 20 years of experience in education. She has authored books, journals, and planners, including The Truth About Affirmations, She's on Purpose: A Self-Assessment, The Meditation Journal, and the 90-Day Life Balance Success Planner. She is also the co-author of several upcoming books.

Dr. Andrews served over 16 years in the K-12 system as a teacher and school principal. She also served as a college professor and is currently the CEO of She's on Purpose. As a Purpose coach she is dedicated to helping women discover their purpose and crush the limiting beliefs that hold them back from prosperous lives.

As a purpose coach, Dr. Andrews has served over 200 clients and helped them live more purposeful lives. Seventy-five percent of clients have discovered their purpose and live happier lives.

Share what you do and your experience with education.

I am an author, speaker, and coach, and I help women discover their purpose and crush the limiting beliefs that hold them back from walking in it. I was a public school teacher for K to 12 for ten years, and I spent another eight years as a principal of a middle-high alternative school which included 6th through 12th graders. Then for another six years I was a college professor teaching teachers.

What is one thing you love the most about being a teacher, or if you are no longer teaching, what do you love most about your new profession?

I'm still teaching, just in a different capacity, but the one thing I love most about teaching really is just to be able to help someone on that journey to discovering, discovering whatever the knowledge is that they're seeking. And that can be from elementary on up, watching kindergarteners discover how to write their name for the first time, or adults, helping adults discover what their purpose is and how to build from that. That whole discovery process is what I really love about teaching.

What are some challenges you've faced as a teacher?

Wow. One of the biggest challenges is being able to stick to prescribed tools to use to meet state requirements or district requirements, when you know your students need something else. So that battle between using materials, curriculum, and things that you know would benefit your students more, as opposed to using district or state-mandated materials. So that was always the most difficult thing for me because I wanted to give my students the best and what I knew that they would benefit from. And sometimes, that was the opposite of what was mandated. And so that struggle was always a real struggle for me.

If you could give two tips to a new teacher reading this book, what would they be?

So the first tip I would give to a teacher is to *believe that what you're doing in the classroom is the right thing for your students.*

You have to be able to have that trust in yourself and that what you're doing is right. Even if it doesn't seem like it's working right now, believe that it is the right thing because that's going to help you stay positive and really fight for what you know your students need. So that would be one tip.

The other tip would be to *find someone that you connect with that's been in the profession that does not mind mentoring you and guiding you and who will also hold you accountable.* Because for me, I found that I really began to find joy in teaching when I had someone who had been doing it longer than me and wasn't afraid to show me how to do what I needed to do and to still feel good about it. So I would say get a mentor ASAP.

Well, if I can throw in a third, it would be to *make sure that you also show up for yourself in the classroom.* In the classroom. And what I mean by that is, a lot of times in the classroom, we're showing up for the district, we're showing up for the principal, we're showing up for our counterparts. But make sure that you show up for yourself in the classroom so that you're not just doing what's required, but that you're getting joy out of it.

If you stayed in the classroom, what motivated you to stay, and what advice would you provide to someone who was in a similar position? Or if you left the classroom, what influenced that decision, and how did you decide your next steps?

I had a couple of transitions from the classroom, from teacher to reading coach then principal. And what ultimately caused me to make that decision was I wanted to make a bigger impact than just on the students that were in the classroom that were assigned to me. I felt like there was only so much I could do in my classroom with my 30 students or however many students. And I knew that I could make a better impact outside the classroom by working directly with teachers. I looked around and saw so many teachers still in survival mode in the classroom after five years of teaching, and I was thriving. I wanted to be able to help more teachers get to that point.

As a teacher, there are only so many other teachers you can really work with. And I figured as a principal, I would have a better opportunity to impart more strategies and different things to teachers that I knew could benefit them and move them from that survival stage of teaching. I just wanted to make a bigger impact, and that's what drew me to becoming a principal. And then, even making that transition from principal to college professor, it was still based on the impact.

I had this desire to help prospective teachers before they got into the classroom, mainly because, as a principal, I found that when teachers move from school to school, they take their school culture with them. And sometimes, it's hard to assimilate into the culture of a new school because each school has its own culture. I wanted to be able to impact teachers before they got into a particular school ecosystem to ensure that they were really prepared to go into any situation and feel confident that they could really thrive there. So that kind of led me from teacher to principal and then to college professor.

Why is a book like this needed?

Wow. If I was a beginning teacher and I had a book like this that was advice from other teachers, I know it would have helped me in those early survival years of teaching. Sometimes it's hard to get real solid advice, especially when you're new to the profession. Everyone tells you, at least in my experience, that you should just assimilate to whatever the district wants and not try to do too much. I found whatever the culture of a particular school is can really affect your effectiveness in the classroom. The need for unfiltered, positive, and helpful advice from others who have gone before you is needed.

And so I feel like a book like this will be able to give so many different perspectives because all of the contributors came from so many different walks of life, you know, so many different cultures. And it's not just this one culture that a teacher will have to assimilate to, but it basically gets a varied amount of advice from different perspectives all in one place. So it's needed even not just for new teachers, but for teachers who might be in that decisive spot, right, who may be feeling that struggle, like, do I stay? Do I go? It gives them something to really ponder on, to think about before they make that decision.

Based on your experience, what would you say to a teacher who is unsure about whether to stay or leave the classroom?

Wow, that's a battle. That is a battle because it was a battle for me because, in one way, you feel like you're leaving your students or you're being disloyal to them, and on the other hand, you're trying to make a bigger impact. I would really just say, for one, make sure that the move is not just about a position, right, or power, or money. Because I mean, how satisfied you are in that position is going to be limited if that's the case. Most teachers are in the classroom because it's really what they love to do.

They love to work with students. I know I found when I first left the class I really missed my students. And I would find myself back in the school all the time because that's really where my heart was connected, even though I knew I wanted to make a bigger impact. So just make sure you're very clear with what it is you desire long-term in your life and what that looks like. And then the second thing I would say is to make sure that wherever you're going to be moving to from the classroom, if you make that decision to leave, make sure that it's going to be able to satisfy a core need of yours.

Because if not, then you're just going to move into a situation where you'll be unhappy because it's not your purpose. And so, you know, make sure that the decision is not just about, like I said, money or a position because the classroom really needs great teachers. I'm always torn between whether teachers should stay or go. But if you lost your zeal for the day-to-day in the classroom, if you feel like you're having more frustrating days than happy days, then I say leave. That should be one of the factors in your decision. Because if the kids aren't bringing you joy, if the classroom isn't bringing you joy, then you're not going to bring joy to the classroom, so leave.

If you had the power to change something in the education system, what would it be and why?

Wow. So I've had the opportunity to change some things, which I'm proud of, and I like that I had the opportunity to work for a charter network and serve schools across the country. I've had the privilege of building a school from the ground up, creating an entirely new education model, which I loved. And so, for me, I think that would be the one thing I would do. I would give schools more autonomy to select the resources they need based on the students they serve.

I guess it's a paradigm shift for each school based on the location that school is in and making a decision about curriculum, everything based on that one particular school, as opposed to looking at things as a district. And I know that is a harder thing to do, but I think it's necessary. So having more school-level teams that make the decisions for that particular school curriculum is important.

As opposed to a district-mandated curriculum, I think that our students are so different, and our students require such individualized education that it's hard to have a cookie-cutter-type school. And I know it's necessary for management reasons, but I think it's definitely doable with the right systems put in place.

So if there was one thing I could change, I would make it so that schools were able to make more school-based decisions and not district-based decisions, especially when it comes to curriculum and instruction.

What is your favorite quote?

Your purpose matters; discover it and take up space!

~ Dr. Dashia Andrews

Martina Britt Yelverton

Instagram - martinabrittyelverton
Facebook - brandmastermartinaby
Linkedin - martinabrittyelverton
martinabrittyelverton.com

Martina Britt Yelverton is known as BrandMaster, Cashflow Queen and Founder of the #1 HireYourKids Legal Tax Hack Movement, #YouthLifestyleTraining. Her daily goal is to Brand You, Educate You and Help You …#GetYoASSetsInOrder. She is your Go2Girl for Simplified Blueprints & Graphics, and she helps people **who want help**! If you're in need of the help she's been blessed to offer, Follow Her **and** Select the Bell for alerts when she "Goes Live" on YouTube or Facebook.

FREE CONTENT is available on her Entrepreneurs Secrets Revealed Mailing list at http://martinabrittyelverton.com. **Speaking of FREE…Grab her free Annual Momentum Planning tool at:** http://momentum.martinabrittyelverton.com

If you've struggled as a **Parent**, as an **Entrepreneur**, or as a **Brand** or **Savvy Senior**, She Can Help You:

- GetYoASSetsInOrder
- Get Branded
- Get Found On Google
- Get Paid Daily &
- Get Published on Amazon

If you're serious, text "brandmaster" to 9198498808 TODAY!

Share what you do and your experience with education.

Thank you so much for that question. My name is BrandMaster Martina Britt Yelverton! I am a BrandMaster, a Cashflow Queen, and the Founder of the #1 Legal Tax Hack to Hire Your Kids in Your Home Based Business, which I've termed Youth Lifestyle Training. That's what/where I teach from. I educate with the mindset to help people understand their own personal value. Whether you are a layperson of the field, an entrepreneur, or a savvy senior, you're probably someone who is out here trying to get an education in entrepreneurship and/or how to start a home-based business. That is my main field of education.

What is one thing you love the most about being a teacher, or if you are no longer teaching, what do you love most about your new profession?

Probably when the light bulb goes on. I love being able to provide a solution. When an individual asks a question and I know that I have the answer and I'm able to visualize what the end result looks like based on the information that's been provided, it makes my heart sing to see the light bulb come on and then to watch that individual pick up whatever that visual that we've just established is and run with it. It gives me joy to know that I've been able to help them move forward with whatever it is they're trying to pursue.

What are some challenges you've faced as a teacher?

Making the realities of this industry plain is not always the most fulfilling, AND also when you feel like you cannot provide a solution. It's a challenge to hear a person's wants or desires and yet realize that they don't really have an established mission or plan to get there. They don't really have a vision for where it is they're trying to go. They're not really sure what their core values are. They haven't set any goals. They haven't put a plan together. So to then have to let that individual know, these are all the foundational aspects that you need to have in place so that you can move... I guess that hard work is the challenge. Because it's the unknown but needed effort and knowledge that you can move forward if you know ahead of time what is needed AND put in the work to get there.

Once this is implemented, you can now have a goal set AND be able to reverse engineer and nearly guarantee meeting that goal. That's been a challenge as well because a lot of people really are not open to how much it actually takes to be an entrepreneur. How much it actually takes to navigate this journey is a HUGE challenge not everyone tells the truth about. When you bring people into the reality of what it is that they "think" they want to do, and when you break it down... what it takes... and you kind of see that light bulb go off or it dims, you're within yourself trying to figure out, now, how do I turn this around so that they are excited again about whatever their goal or vision is. THAT'S A CHALLENGE!

If you could give two tips to a new teacher reading this book, what would they be?

Number one, ***stay open, read the book, and find yourself in the book***. When you take up this book, you read the title of this book, and you get excited about knowing that there is a story in this book that may potentially set you free... just stay open to the information that all of the co-authors are providing. Next, read the book and then find yourself in these pages and be ready to be set free to make a decision as to whether or not you're going to stay in the classroom or leave the classroom - or do both.

I'll say again, stay open and realize that your story is somewhere in the book. Just be open because a lot of times, you read things guarded, so you're not really open. You can't absorb the information that's being distributed if you're closed!

The second thing was to *actually complete the book.* We pick up books sometimes and we don't complete them. We'll start, we'll read one or two chapters, and we won't complete them. So I would say read each individual story over time, find yourself in it, stay open to that person's account of their experience, and then navigate your journey based on the tips that are given by my other co-authors.

What motivated you to stay, and what advice would you provide to someone who was in a similar position?

Well, virtually, it's nice to be able to be in your natural habitat. That is one of the things that I would hope people would understand about being able to be virtual or being able to be outside of the classroom and being in your natural habitat to be able to teach from because, to me, it makes you more genuine. And because I'm able to do that and I'm able to offer and lend to the field what it is that I have to offer from my natural habitat, experiences, and real-world examples. It makes it convenient, yes, but it makes it comfortable enough to be able to really be me and really give from my heart everything that's been purposed inside me. To give to the field or to give to a participant, or to give to a student who wants to learn from me.

Being virtual, being in my natural habitat, allows us to be really authentic. And to me, it allows us to go much deeper to get to the core of what it is that I'm trying to establish with my students so that they can feel really confident about moving forward and what we've established. There are distractions and challenges here in our natural habitat, and we can give solutions to even overcome those as well.

Why is a book like this needed?

Because you need different perspectives, I feel a book like this is really important because you get to see different perspectives on different topics. You can find yourself somewhere in there. You can become familiar with someone, you can get to know someone's story, and you can get to know different aspects of why the "thing is a thing" and why that "thing" makes sense to you. And also, you get to understand you're not alone. You know, when you hear other people and when they're speaking, you're like, "yeah, that makes sense," or, "I thought I was the only one," you're able to relate to them. It allows you, as I said earlier, to stay open and to remain open to hear the end of their journey and to live a little bit vicariously through them.

Based on your experience, what would you say to a teacher who is unsure about whether to stay or leave the classroom?

I would say to get 100% dialed into two things. Number one, **your** goal, **your** end result, **your** purpose, settle into that so that you can authentically show up in the classroom or so that you can know that the classroom is not your best place to educate from. So that you can know that whatever it is that you've been purposed here to do, you are enough to do that. You have everything you need inside of you to do exactly what it is that you have been purposed here to do.

If you dial 100% into that, it will help you make a decision whether or not receiving education from you inside of a classroom during formal education is what's best for those that you have been purposed/called to serve. To really know and understand who needs what it is that you've been blessed to give them so that you can determine where those individuals are. Whether they're in the world or whether they're in the classroom, and then by knowing who you are, you could show up, and by knowing who you're here to serve, you can actually serve them and give them what it is that they need.

If you had the power to change something in the education system, what would it be and why?

I'm really excited about this question because the number one thing that I would change if I had the power to change the education system would be to change two things.

I would change the structure of it because we're in a different world now. We're in a different world from when I came up in the classroom, and I learned the five WS: the who, what, the when, the where, and the why. I learned in a structured manner AND for the time that I was living in. I feel much of the curriculum, although it has evolved, I do not feel that a lot of what is being taught is actually preparing people for the world or preparing kids to become people for the world that we're actually living in now.

I would want that curriculum, that structure, those confines, those four walls that curriculum operates in, to be really studied. And even though we have evolved, it really needs to become even more of what is actually needed for a specific type of child. And yes, you can't please everyone, but you can expand the curriculum so that it includes and that it allows a person to really learn and thrive the way that **they** need to, for whatever they are purposed to do. That's number one.

And two, *I would ensure that the coins match!* This is a very hard arena to be in, to try to take a person's programming that they've grown up with and to try to shape that programming and that education that they're learning from, and not be compensated to a point where you're able to take care of yourself. I've known teachers who work all day, who have a part-time job, and then end up hustling as well just to be able to make ends meet. Educators should be HIGHLY compensated for their passion. And we have some really passionate teachers, formal teachers, and nonformal teachers. We have really passionate educators. And I would love it if the compensation for even the formal teaching would really match a lot of the entertainment or even the medical field because it is crucially important. It's just as important, if not more, than innovation in medical, technological, and environmental fields, hands down!

Angela Taylor

Instagram - lcbtutoring
Linkedin - angela-taylor
www.lcbtutoring.com

Angela Taylor is from Dallas, Texas. She graduated from Stephen F. Austin State University with a degree in Education. When Angela received her bachelor's degree in Education, she just knew she would spend the rest of her life teaching in the classroom, impacting students and their families! This vision of wanting to make a strong difference in the world of education began in Pre-K after she had a phenomenal teacher, Mrs. Shields, who helped her FALL IN LOVE with learning at such a young age, which inspired her to become a teacher! In the middle of Angela's 3rd year of teaching, she left the classroom due to growing tired of toxic Administrators who were sucking the joy and love out of teaching for her. She overcame this obstacle by building a closer relationship with God and Jesus to help her embrace a different purpose, and starting her own tutoring businesses that she named after her uncle, Luther Charles Bradley. She started her businesses to be able to help students and make a difference in their lives without all the demands and toxic leadership she experienced in her few years of being in the classroom. This helped bring the joy back to teaching for her, and this is only the beginning. She currently owns two businesses, LCB Tutoring and LCB Coaching. Her mission is to help inspire young students to fall in love with learning and bring the joy back to learning, while also helping them manage their Executive Function Challenges with ease and confidence. She also wants to help educators realize how special they truly are. Angela loves quotes, but one of her favorite quotes is by Eleanor Roosevelt : "Do something everyday that scares you."

Share what you do and your experience with education.

My experience with education has definitely been a rollercoaster ride, but looking back, I am thankful for each part of the journey. I'll start from the beginning. I received my bachelor's degree in Education in December 2017, and I began teaching the following month in January 2018. Although I loved teaching my students and their parents, I quickly became burnt out within my first three years of teaching. I became so burnt out that I quit my last teaching job on March 1, 2021. Let me be clear, I was not burnt out by my students; they are actually the reason I stayed as long as I did. It was due to having a toxic principal and all the demands outside of teaching, but don't worry; I will get to that later.

I've always loved teaching. It's been my passion since I was in Pre-K, thanks to my teacher Mrs. Shields who helped me fall in love with learning at such a young age. I remember wanting to be just like her as a kid, like, I literally have a picture of myself dressed up as a teacher. I have experience with third and fourth-grade reading and writing. I also taught first grade for one year. Right now, I am currently teaching and coaching within my two online businesses called LCB Tutoring and LCB Coaching. I also plan to create other businesses to impact education in the future.

What is one thing you love the most about being a teacher, or if you are no longer teaching, what do you love most about your new profession?

One thing that I love the most is really helping those kids that come to me, and they don't have any confidence, or they don't believe in themselves, or they don't feel like they're smart or good enough. I feel like that's one of the parts that I love the most because I remember when I was growing up, I felt that way. I was always really smart, but mentally, I just didn't feel included. I didn't feel "there," if that makes sense. The social-emotional part of teaching is something that I really cling to a lot, and just helping my students to gain confidence is one of my favorite parts of teaching.

What are some challenges you've faced as a teacher?

I'm going to be honest, it's been a lot, and none of it has to do with the children. The kids are always the best part. I'll talk about my top two challenges I faced as a teacher.

One of them has been that I have had *very poor Admin at the schools that I have worked at, along with what I feel to be, at times, unrealistic demands for one person to handle alone.* This is coming from a teacher who was very new to the profession. I felt some burn-out after my 1st full year. During my last teaching job, the stress got so real that I began to have high blood pressure consistently, and my mental health suffered so much that I had no choice but to quit to save myself; that is how I felt. And I'm in my 20s, by the way, so that's not really normal to have that consistently. I had a lot of anxiety. Stress. And I felt so much pressure, especially when I was teaching in Texas.

The kids have to have a certain test score. This led me to my second challenge. *My joy for teaching was being taken away because I kept feeling like every day when I went into the class,* I was preparing them for a test every day. And it was just so much pressure. And I wasn't enjoying it. I'm going to be even more transparent and tell you that I was starting to hate teaching because I felt like I was teaching to a test, and I felt so much toxic energy from principals and just the people that were above the principal that was transferring that toxic energy down, and it was coming to us, teachers. I loved my students and I did not want to 100% lose my passion for teaching, so I quit. The sad part is, my last principal knew I was a great teacher. As soon as I put in my two weeks notice, he set up a meeting asking me to stay, but I could not take the stress anymore and I stood my ground on leaving. On my last day back in March of 2021, I remember he called the police on me due to being angry about me moving my things out of the classroom in the middle of the day, and this was already pre-planned. I prayed that day, and God gave me a supernatural peace that I cannot explain, and I kept pushing through even with the police watching me. The good news is the police knew he was being petty, even though they did not say it, and I had emails to prove that it was my move-out day. As rapper Jay-Z says, *"Things don't happen to you, they happen for you."*

If you could give two tips to a new teacher reading this book, what would they be?

One tip that I have for a new teacher, and I wish somebody would have told me this is, as basic as it may sound is; You are very gifted and talented in a lot of different areas. I think sometimes when we are teachers, we feel like, okay, we're here to teach the kids, but start really paying attention to yourself and start really taking time to figure out other strengths that you have as well that are a result of your teaching. By doing this, you can tap into so many other gifts that you have as well and really see how much of a superhero you really are. Although I was humble, I always knew I was a great teacher, but when I left teaching, I began to also realize that teaching taught me how to multi-task, have supernatural patience, customer service, and so many other valuable skills I was able to carry over into my tutoring businesses.

You may be really good at multitasking, interacting with people, or connecting with others. I recommend really starting to look into some of your other strengths, too. I think sometimes, as teachers, we forget that we also have other strengths that can also be an addition, and we can use them in other areas that are related to teaching as well. I want you to continue to pay attention to your strengths and remind yourself of how good you are, because that's going to help you a lot in the classroom to keep yourself uplifted.

And I would say the second tip that I have is to establish a work-life balance, with self-care from the beginning. I recommend creating strict boundaries to protect yourself. Do not get in the habit of taking your laptop home, doing lesson plans at home, etc. I feel like the best way to continue to enjoy teaching and continue to get the most out of it and be present when you're there is to have a work-life balance. Keep "work" at "work." Leave your classroom at work as much as you can so that when you go home, you can be home.

If you stayed in the classroom, what motivated you to stay, and what advice would you provide to someone who was in a similar position? Or if you left the classroom, what influenced that decision, and how did you decide your next steps?

I'll just kind of share why I left in the beginning and kind of my current status of how I feel about staying now.

One of the main reasons why I left the classroom is because of the principal at my last school in Dallas ISD. I had a really great assistant principal, though. The staff was great, and the kids were great. But the regular principal, he was the reason why I left, because it was so much negative energy. I just felt like every time we tried to have fun with the kids, he would get very upset. He wanted the class to always be quiet. We couldn't have recess. I was teaching fourth graders; they need to have recess, and they need to have fun. He would come in throwing stuff sometimes, like, if he saw the kids not getting ready or doing something kind of getting off task a little bit, he would come in with such negative energy. And because of his toxicity, disrespectfulness, and all of the name callings, I decided that it was time for me to leave. And honestly, I didn't feel guilty about it. I prayed about it before it happened, and I planned my exit, because my health was starting to go down so much. I cried every day and ½ the night.

It was either I had to choose my health or teaching. I remember my doctor had told me that. So I chose my health, and I left. What made it a lot easier, though, was that I had a really good relationship with my students and their parents, so I could call and FaceTime them, and they knew the principal, and how his behavior was. My students and their parents supported my decision to leave, and I still got to see them. This helped me not feel guilty when I did leave because I had a big support system.

Now, I am teaching online in my tutoring business, and my passion for teaching has been restored. I feel empowered and at peace with my decision, and I have no plans of going back in the classroom, if it is God's will.

Why is a book like this needed?
I feel like a book like this is so needed because I mean, even if you're not in a school or you haven't been in education, but you might be thinking about it, or whatever the case may be, people are seeing all over the country the teacher shortage right now and how teachers are just leaving the classroom. Many teachers are wondering if they should go into the classroom or if they shouldn't. And I feel like a book like this is needed because I think it's important for all teachers to be able to decide if they should leave or go into the classroom, but they should get it from multiple perspectives because I'm very unbiased when it comes to it. I've had both, you know, and I'm currently kind of living both.

So I feel like it is important for teachers to just kind of know what they're getting into to make the best decision and to really decide. Is this for me? Should I do this? Teachers should look at the pros and cons of different educators and hear their stories, because I know if I had a book like this before I started teaching, it would have helped me to feel a lot more prepared, I'll say, because a lot of stuff that happened, I wasn't ready for.

I think a book like this can just really give it from multiple perspectives so you can make the best decision for you whether you decide to go or not.

Based on your experience, what would you say to a teacher who is unsure about whether to stay or leave the classroom?
I would say this can be tricky because I feel you have to make the best decision for you, and I am so open-minded that it is hard for me to give a solid answer. I feel like we should listen to the

thing that we often ignore, and it's our gut feeling. I feel like you should just really listen to your gut. I feel like your gut is also God's way of talking to you. If you're going to look up information about why you should go into the classroom, don't just look up the negative or don't just look up the positive. Look up a variety of different sources, but listen to your gut and think about what is best for you.

Don't make a decision by being influenced by other people. Not to say that you shouldn't listen to other people's experiences, but their experiences might not be yours. For example, I shared my negative experiences with the admin but positive ones with the kids;you may never have this experience. Your journey may look totally different.

Listen to your gut and just train your mind to get comfortable with being uncomfortable. Because whether you decide to stay or leave the classroom, both feelings can sometimes be uncomfortable. But just continue to listen to your gut. Pray about it. If prayer is a part of what you do, and if you do decide to stay in the classroom, I would just say that that's always great because we do need teachers.

Make sure that you are taking care of yourself, practicing self-care, keeping things balanced, and just really paying attention to the culture of the school. The good part about teaching now is we can be a little bit pickier because there are so many openings available, so find a school you feel goes with your morals and values. It's okay to be picky if that's what you need to do to do what's best for you as far as staying or leaving and picking a school.

If you do decide to leave from my perspective, I would say just always make sure you have a backup plan. From my experience, having a backup plan made the transition much easier. What are you going to do financially and with yourself? The last thing you want to do is leave the classroom and then just become idle because that can bring about some different emotions and cause you to make unhealthy decisions. One other tip is to have a supportive community around you. Don't talk to people that are closed-minded. I made that mistake by telling some family members who thought I was crazy for leaving, and that can make you feel worse. Luckily, I had a very supportive husband in my corner the whole time to talk to. You want to talk to people that are open-minded and that are going to be positive towards whatever you decide to do.

If you had the power to change something in the education system, what would it be and why?

I would say that if I had the power to change one thing, I would change toxic leadership, toxic admin, and toxic principals that exist at some schools. It's micromanaging, being unsupportive, treating teachers without kindness, having super-long meetings, and all of these obligations that we have that become so stressful. For example, our contracts are from eight to three, but it can turn into us working from eight to six, eight to seven if we're not careful. That's toxic. That's not healthy, and that's not going to keep a teacher motivated and feeling well and showing up best for her students.

If I could change one thing, it would be toxic leadership. We need people to be leaders, not just because of their degree, but who actually know how to value feedback and not take it as a way to retaliate. We also need leaders who are going to support teachers, listen to teachers, give us more time to prepare, and stop adding unnecessary stuff to our plate, and just allow us to be for the kids. This is why this would be the one thing I would change.

Acknowledgments

Vernon Hargrove
Harmoni Clark
Luther-Charles Bradley
Bobbie Bradley

Conclusion

I hope you enjoyed this book as much as I enjoyed creating it. This vision was one that I had to bring to life, and I am so blessed that I was able to partner with so many people in order to make this book a reality. My hope is that you will no longer feel alone because you will be able to relate to someone's story within the pages. Whether you are working in education or working in another profession, you may have contemplated at one time or another whether you should stay or leave.

To Teach or Not to Teach provided you with many stories and tips from real people who encountered different experiences while in the educational space. Every story shared is unique, and I'm sure you were able to relate with at least one of these authors.

And if you are reading as a parent/guardian of a child who goes to school, then I hope you were able to get a better insight into some of the things your child's teacher might be experiencing.

You took the time to read and learn more about this controversial topic because you understand the importance of education and how all over the world, many educators are asking themselves if they want to continue to teach. No one's story is more important than another; everyone has a unique experience and perspective when it comes to education.

If you are a teacher and you have a story to share with the world, just like these amazing co-authors in this book, then I hope you understand your voice needs to be heard.

Ways to Connect:

If you are interested in checking out some of our Free & Paid Resources to get you started with sharing your story, then scan the QR Code Below to connect with me.

If you know you are ready to publish your book then head to books2impact.com

If you enjoyed this book, be sure to leave a review on what you thought about our book on Amazon.

Love,
The Visionary Author Shanine Alessia Young

Book Shanine to Speak

Shanine Alessia Young is a World Renowned Author, Professional Speaker, Coach and Certified Educator.

Shanine has over 10+ years of experience in public speaking, teaching and coaching. She is passionate about inspiring students, leaders and educators on how to increase their impact and confidence.

For more information and to book Shanine to speak at your next event please visit shaninealessia.com

Some of her Speaking Presentations are listed below:

- Freedom Over Fear (How to Overcome Your Fears & Achieve Your Goals)
- Reaching & Teaching In and Out of the Classroom (Educator Training)
- It's Okay to Be Different (Social-emotional Presentation for Kids)
- Turn Your Story into Profit (Book Publishing & Marketing)

For more information and to book Shanine to speak at your next event please visit shaninealessia.com

Bonus Material

Do you have your copy?

Reaching While Teaching: An Educator's Guide to Impacting & Transforming Lives.

Available on Amazon

Bonus Material

Inspiring Words from an Educator

Why did I choose to teach?

I chose to make my classroom a world of wonder for my students, where they feel safe, happy, and comfortable exploring different ways to learn.

Teaching is a calling; everything you do with love will significantly impact the lives of others, and that's why I teach.

Here are a few tips to keep you teaching:

1- Develop strong relationships/trust with students and parents.
2- Do what's best for you and the kids while still complying with standards.
3- Keep the kids engaged by establishing student ownership. Accountability is huge when students are in charge of their learning by giving them responsibilities and jobs and using student role models from your class.
4- Use hands-on resources combined with music and movement.
5- Make your classroom a fun and happy place to be.

Silvana Spence
Jacksonville, Florida

Bonus Teacher Resources

1. **Teachercreated.com-** Teacher Created Resources is an educational publishing company created by teachers for teachers and parents.

2. **Teacherspayteachers.com-** Teachers Pay Teachers is an online marketplace where teachers buy and sell original educational materials.

3. **Oriental Trading-** A Platform perfect for teachers looking for the ultimate collection of teaching resources, classroom decorations, and school supplies.

4. **Ted-ED-** Includes a collection of high-quality, interactive, video-based lessons on a daily basis for free. These are available in every subject and grade level.

5. **KeepingTeachersTeaching.org-** A non-profit organization devoted to the needs of teachers. They raise funding to assist teachers.

6. **Deavionbluinnovations.com-** A black-owned business that specializes in cute teacher fashion made by a teacher for teachers.

7. **Ten Tribe for Teachers Facebook group-** A group created to celebrate sisterhood among black and brown women in education. We are here to mentor, uplift, and empower women to continue to be passionate about education.

8. **Beconnectededconsulting.com-** Provides school & district level consulting to organizations based on our C.R.A.D.L.E. Framework. They also provide coaching & mentoring through their TeacHER Empowerment Network.

9. **Teaching Queen Collective-** Helping fellow teachers and teacherpreneurs save time and money by creating useful and engaging resources in Canva.

Business Listings

Life's Beautiful Diamonds

Shawnda Louise Michael

But thou shalt remember the Lord thy God; for it is He that giveth thee power to get wealth, that He may establish His covenant which He swore unto thy fathers, as it is this day. Deuteronomy 8:18.

Our experience enables us to offer effective individualized, health, beauty and self care. We are here to empower and transform you into a sparkling diamond. diamonds counseling beautiful.

Edwards Administrative and Bookkeeping Services, LLC

LaTonia Brown-Edwards

I can do all things through Christ who strengthens me!!

We are a full service Bookkeeping, Accounting, and Tax Business. We specialize in individual and small business needs and services

King Kemari, LLC

Shandelle Stewart

With God all things are possible.

A company derived from a reformed mindset. We urge our clients to walk an uplifting path with a prolific mindset.

Blessed and Beautiful International

Princess Millens

Proverbs 16:3 AMP

Commit your works to the LORD [submit and trust them to Him], And your plans will succeed [if you respond to His will and guidance].

Hi Everyone! I am Princess, mother of three wonderful children, an educator, a bestselling author, a minister of the Gospel, an empowerment speaker, Podcast host and committed to serving people in need.

Eminflow Music Studio

Emily Ballhouse
"Bear one another's burdens, and so fulfill the law of Christ."
Galatians 6:2 NKJV

I am a piano teacher, Recording Artist, poet and author of 'Only You - The Poems'. I songwrite and produce my vocals (although I do enlist help when I can afford it!) and when I learn how to do something new, I seem to have a habit of teaching others to do the same, such as registering their music for royalty collection with the appropriate metadata! If I can help you come up, I will. If you want to know something about relationships and God, check out my book and listen to my music. I'm Canadian, but the internet makes lots of things possible. I have my own studio gear, so if you ever want to collab, I'm your girl. I have a background in opera, but my vibe these days is RnB/Pop in the Christian Hip Hop arena. I've homeschooled my daughter, Naomi who is now in grade 4, since day 1. If you have any questions about it, I'd love to hear from you!

Stephanie Speaks

Stephanie Williams

We just need to look pass our own understanding and tap into a whole new dimension. Which will allow you to no longer be blind to the your true identity and your purpose on earth.
(Proverbs 3:5-6)

Stephanie Williams is the CEO and Founder of Stephanie Speaks, Destined to Conquer. She is a published author, motivational speaker and transformational divorce coach. She has been a featured leading expert in the media, video, and interviews. Stephanie is passionate about empowering her audiences and clients with her step-by-step systems so they can release the past pain and hurt, to remove the 'victim' mentality and replace it with a 'warrior' mentality. So they can be able to see the power that's within them.

Kingdom KEYS Mentoring

Charles Osuji

Joshua 1:9

9 Have I not commanded you? Be strong and courageous. Do not be afraid; do not be discouraged, for the Lord your God will be with you wherever you go.

We are a college & career readiness teen program designed to help guide middle & high school students manage internal conflict when it comes to picking the right career, college, and major by connecting those major decisions with their gifts & talents. By doing this we believe that it can lead to significant increase in student academics, confidence, and behavior.